Baby Girl Names

D1188969

Jane Nyah

Quantum Theory Media

Table of Contents

HOW TO USE THIS DICTIONARY

Thank you for purchasing Baby Girl Names and welcome! You must be excited about the arrival of your daughter. Let me start out by saying congratulations!

Using this dictionary is easy and we have split the book into two different sections depending on how you want to choose the name of your child.

Section One : Sorted By Name

The first half of the book sorts the names from A to Z. For example:

Aaliyah: ascending or rising (Hebrew); lofty (Arabic)

The first name in the book is Aaliyah. This book has 2 different meanings. It means ascending or rising in Hebrew and lofty in Arabic. In most cases these meanings are not literal translations; they are derivates. That is, they derive their meaning from a common root word.

To use section one, simply browse through the list of names and highlight any that you like. Shortlist those that have a meaning that you find of interest.

Section Two : Sorted By Meaning

The second half of the book sorts the name by meaning.

To use this section, scroll through the definitions and highlight any that you like. For example, if you wanted to associate your child's name with the word *strong*, then all you need to do is turn to the S section in latter half and browse through the 25 names listed under this definition:

strong: *Abira, Adira, Ethana (Hebrew), Alima (Arabic), Andria, Andriana, Valentina, Valentine, Valerie, Valonia, Valora (Latin), Bernice (Greek), Breana, Bria, Byanna (Celtic), Anrette, Arnelle, Bernadette, Bernadine (French), Carlotta (Italian), Charla (English), Charmaine (German), Lera (Russian), Valencia (Spanish), Waleria (Polish)*

Remember to take your time when choosing a name. After all, it will last your daughter a lifetime

SORTED BY NAMES A – Z

A

Aaliyah: ascending or rising (Hebrew); lofty (Arabic)

Aasta: love (Nordic)

Abbey: lay-abbot, someone who worked in a monastery (Scottish); her father rejoiced (Hebrew)

Abena: born on Tuesday (Ghanaian)

Abigail: father's joy, fountain of joy (Hebrew)

Abira: brave, strong (Hebrew)

Acacia: spiny, thorn (Greek); honorable (Spanish)

Acima: praised by God (Hebrew)

Ada: noble, noble birth (Latin)

Adalia: noble (German); Yahweh is just (Hebrew)

Adama: beautiful child (African); red earth (Latin)

Adara: beautiful young girl (Greek); purity (Arabic); renowned (Hebrew)

Adela: noble (German)

Adelaide: noble (German)

Adena: decoration (Hebrew)

Adiel: ornament of the Lord (Hebrew)

Adina: delicate, gentle, noble (Hebrew)

Adira: powerful, strong (Hebrew)

Adonica: sweet (Spanish)

Adonia: very attractive (Greek)

Adora: adorable, beautiful (Latin)

Adorlee: adored, greatly loved (Greek)

Adorna: beautiful woman (Greek); decorated with jewels (Latin)

Adria: from Hadria (Greek)

Adriana: from Hadria (Greek)

Adriane: from Hadria (Greek)

Aerona: berry (Welsh)

Afina: young deer (Hebrew)

Agatha: kind, good (Greek)

Aglaia: brilliant beauty (Greek)

Agnes: pure, holy (Greek)

Aharona: enlightened (Hebrew); messenger (Arabic)

Ahuda: friendship, peaceful (Hebrew)

Ahulani: heavenly shrine (Hawaiian)

Ahyoka: bringer of happiness (Native American)

Aida: helpful (Latin); reward (Arabic)

Aileen: shining light (Irish)

Ailsa: cheerful girl (German)

Aine: joy, fire (Irish)

Ainsley: from the meadow clearing, clearing (English)

Airlea: ethereal (Greek)

Aisha: alive and well (Arabic); life (Swahili)

Aissa: vision, dream (Gaelic)

Aiyana: always flowering (Native American)

Aja: goat (Hindi)

Akako: red (Japanese)

Akala: parrot (Aboriginal)

Akela: noble (Hawaiian)

Aki: Autumn (Japanese)

Akiko: bright child (Japanese)

Akilah: intelligent (Arabic)

Akili: intelligent (Arabic)

Alaina: bright, happy (Celtic); shining light (German)

Alana: handsome, harmony, happy, peaceful (Hawaiian)

Alannah: handsome, harmony, happy, peaceful (Hawaiian)

Alani: orange tree (Hawaiian); precious (German)

Alanis: beautiful, bright child (Irish); precious (German)

Alarice: noble, regal ruler (German)

Alaula: dawn (Hawaiian)

Alba: noble, industrious, bright, famous (English); white (Latin)

Albina: white (Latin)

Alcina: strong minded, sorceress (Greek)

Alda: old, wise, prosperous (German)

Aleah: ascending or rising (Hebrew); from the meadow (English)

Aleela: she cries (Swahili)

Aleena: alone (Dutch); light (Greek)

Aleka: noble (Hawaiian); defender of man (Greek)

Alena: shining light (Russian); tower (Hebrew)

Alesia: helper (Greek)

Aleta: free to travel about (Greek); winged (Latin)

Alethea: truth or truthful one (Greek)

Alex: defender of man (Greek)

Alexandra: defender of man (Greek)

Alexis: defender of man (Greek)

Alice: truthful (Greek); noble (German)

Alicia: truthful (Greek); noble (German)

Alida: beautifully dressed (Greek); small winged one (Latin)

Alika: most beautiful (Nigerian)

Alima: cultured, strong (Arabic)

Alina: bright, beautiful, light (Slavic); harmonious, fair haired (Celtic)

Alisa: happiness, joy (Hebrew)

Alison: Alice's son, son of the little truthful one (Irish); noble (German)

Allison: Alice's son, son of the little truthful one (Irish); noble (German)

Aliya: ascending or rising (Hebrew)

Aliza: joy, happiness (Hebrew)

Alina: light (Slavic); moon (Aboriginal)

Ally: little truthful one (Greek); noble, bright, famous (German)

Alma: kind young woman (Arabic)

Almeta: ambitious (Latin)

Almira: famous, noble (English); princess (Arabic)

Almita: ambitious (Latin)

Alnaba: war (Native American)

Alona: solitary angel, oak tree (Latin)

Aloysia: famous warrior (German)

Alta: majestic, high, elevated (Latin)

Althea: healing, healthy, wholesome (Greek)

Alula: first born (Arabic)

Alura: divine counsellor or adviser (English)

Alva: white (Latin); elf (Swedish)

Alvera: truthful (Latin)

Alvina: elf, magical being, friend to all (English)

Alyssa: sensible, yellow flower (Greek)

Ama: born on a Saturday (Ghanaian)

Amabel: lovable (Latin)

Amada: greatly loved (Spanish)

Amalea: industrious, eager, striving (German)

Amaline: industrious, striving, work (German)

Amanda: lovable (Latin)

Amara: everlasting, eternal beauty (Latin)

Amarina: rain (Aboriginal)

Amarinda: long-lived, everlasting (Greek)

Amaris: promise by God (Hebrew)

Amaryllis: fresh stream, sparkling (Greek)

Amaya: raining at night (Japanese)

Ambel: lovable (Latin)

Amber: semi-precious gem, jewel (Arabic); light (Egyptian)

Ambrosia: immortal (Greek)

Amelia: hard-working, industrious (German)

Amelinda: beautiful, beloved (Spanish)

Amethyst: beneficent, purple gemstone (Greek)

Amice: greatly loved, loved friend (Latin)

Aminta: defender, protector (Greek)

Amira: princess (Arabic)

Amita: truthful, friendship (Hebrew)

Amity: friendly, harmony (Latin)

Ammu: loved aunt (Arabic)

Amorette: little love (French)

Amrita: little love (Spanish)

Amy: greatly loved (Latin)

Ana: God is gracious (Spanish) (Hebrew)

Anais: graceful (Hebrew)

Anala: fine (Hindi)

Ananda: ultimate bliss, joy (Sanskrit)

Ananke: necessity (Greek)

Anastasia: resurrection, springtime (Greek)

Anatolia: eastern (Greek)

Andra: breath (Norse); manly (Greek)

Andria: brave, courageous, strong (Latin); manly (Greek)

Andriana: brave, courageous, strong (Latin); manly (Greek)

Aneira: honorable (Welsh)

Aneko: eldest sister (Japanese)

Anela: angel (Hebrew)

Angel: angel, messenger of God (Greek)

Angelina: angel, messenger of God (Greek)

Angeline: angel, messenger of God (Greek)

Anh: flower (Vietnamese)

Ani: beautiful (Hawaiian); grace (Polish)

Ania: God is gracious (Hebrew)

Aniela: graceful (Hebrew); messenger of God (Greek)

Anika: graceful (Hebrew / Swedish); sweet faced (African)

Anila: God of the wind (Hebrew)

Anisah: friendly, pleasant companion (Arabic)

Anita: graceful (Hebrew)

Anja: graceful (Russian); God has favored me (Hebrew)

Ann: God has favored me (Hebrew)

Anna: God has favored me (Hebrew)

Anne: God has favored me (Hebrew)

Annabella: God has favored me (Hebrew); graceful, lovable, beautiful woman (French / Latin)

Annabelle: God has favored me (Hebrew); graceful, lovable, beautiful woman (French / Latin)

Anneka: graceful (Dutch / Hebrew); sweet faced (African)

Annelise: graceful (German); graced with God's bounty (Latin)

Annetta: God has favored me (Hebrew)

Annette: God has favored me (Hebrew)

Annina: graceful (Hebrew)

Annisa: graceful (Greek)

Annmarie: God has favored me (Hebrew)

Annona: Roman goddess (Greek)

Annora: honor (Latin); shining light (Greek)

Anona: ninth child, yearly crops, pineapple (Latin)

Anthea: flowery (Greek)

Antoinette: priceless (French)

Antonia: priceless (French)

Anya: graceful (Hebrew / Russian)

Aolani: heavenly cloud (Hawaiian)

Aphrodite: goddess of love (Greek)

Apoline: sunlight (Greek)

April: born in April, April (Latin)

Ara: goddess of vengeance (Greek); brings rain (Arabic)

Arabella: asked for, beautiful, prayerful (Latin); eagle (German)

Ardelia: glowing (Latin); blooming meadow (Hebrew)

Ardella: enthusiastic (Latin); blooming meadow (Hebrew)

Arden: great forest (Latin)

Ardis: eager (Latin)

Ardith: field of flowers (Latin)

Arella: angel, messenger of God (Hebrew)

Areta: best, excellence (Greek)

Aretha: best, excellence (Greek)

Aria: melody, song (Italian)

Ariadna: holy (Greek)

Ariadne: holy (Greek)

Ariana: holy (Latin); silver (Welsh)

Arica: ruler (Scandinavian)

Ariel: lioness of God (Hebrew)

Ariella: lioness of God (Hebrew)

Arietta: melody (Italian)

Arika: water lily (Aboriginal); ruler (Norse)

Arlene: promise (Gaelic)

Armida: little armed warrior (Latin)

Armilla: warrior who wears a bracelet in battle (Latin)

Armina: warrior, soldier (German)

Arminda: of high degree (Latin)

Armine: faithful (Hebrew); high ranking (Latin); soldier (German)

Arnelle: powerful, strong (French / Latin)

Anrette: powerful, strong (French / Latin)

Arnina: enlightened singing, mountain or strength (Hebrew)

Arora: cockatoo (Aboriginal)

Artemis: moon goddess (Greek)

Arva: pastures, seashore (Latin)

Asa: born in the morning (Japanese); healer, doctor (Hebrew); goddess (Norse)

Aselma: fair haired (Gaelic)

Ash: ash tree (English)

Asha: life (Swahili); truth (Persian); alive and well (Arabic)

Ashanti: life (Swahili)

Ashia: life, hope (Arabic)

Ashira: wealthy, rich (Hebrew)

Ashley: ash tree meadow (English)

Aspen: aspen tree (English)

Asperity: sharp tempered (English)

Asta: star, star like, love (Greek)

Aster: flower (Greek)

Astera: star like (Greek)

Asteria: star like (Greek)

Astra: star (Latin)

Astria: star (Latin)

Astrid: star (Latin); divine strength (Norse)

Ata: dawn, twilight (Tongan)

Atalaya: guardian (Spanish); watchtower (Arabic)

Atara: diadem, crown (Hebrew)

Athalia: praise God (Hebrew)

Athanasia: immortal, eternal life (Greek)

Athela: noble (German)

Athena: goddess of wisdom (Greek)

Aubery: brown hair, powerful, wise, leader (French); elf, magical being (German)

Audrey: noble strength (English)

Aulani: royal messenger (Hawaiian)

Aura: distinctive air (Greek); Gentle breeze (Latin)

Aurel: golden (Latin)

Aurelia: golden (Latin)

Aurora: goddess of dawn (Greek)

Autumn: Autumn, fall, season of harvest (Latin)

Ava: birdlike (Latin); eagle (Greek)

Avara: youngest child (Sanskrit)

Aveline: hazel nut (German)

Avena: field of oats (Latin)

Averil: boar battle (English)

Avery: confirmation (French); elf counsel (English)

Avice: birdlike (Latin); sanctuary in battle (German); warrior (French)

Avis: sanctuary in battle (English); bird (Latin)

Avoca: sweet valley (Irish)

Avoka: avocado (Tongan)

Avril: born in April, boar warrior woman (English); to open (Latin)

Awena: poetry (Welsh)

Aya: swift bird (Hebrew); woven silk (Japanese)

Ayanna: innocent (Hindi); beautiful flower (Swahili)

Ayasha: life (Persian)

Ayesha: youngest child (Arabic); small one (Persian)

Ayita: first to dance (Cherokee)

Ayla: deer (Hebrew)

Aza: comforting (Arabic)

Azalea: dry earth (Greek); flower (English)

Azariah: God helps, blesses (Hebrew)

Azelia: helped by God (Hebrew); not jealous (Greek)

Azura: blue lapis, gemstone (Persian); sky blue (Spanish)

B

Babette: little stranger (Greek)

Bailey: bailiff (French); berry clearing, city fortification (English)

Bakana: look out, guardian, view (Aboriginal)

Bakula: flower (Hindi)

Bambra: mushroom (Aboriginal)

Bandi: prisoner (Arabic)

Baptisa: one who baptizes (Latin)

Bara: dawn, sunrise (Aboriginal); to select, innocent (Hebrew)

Barbara: stranger (Latin); thorn (English)

Barite: girl (Aboriginal)

Basha: stranger (Polish)

Basia: God's daughter (Hebrew); foreign woman or stranger (Polish)

Basillia: majestic, royal (Greek)

Bathanny: good day (Aboriginal)

Bathilda: woman warrior (German)

Bathsheba: seventh daughter, daughter of oath (Hebrew)

Batul: palm tree shoot (Arabic)

Bea: brings joy and happiness (Latin)

Beatrice: brings joy and happiness (Latin)

Beata: blessed, happy (Latin)

Beca: white, bound, faithful (Slavic)

Becky: white, bound, faithful (Slavic)

Beda: female warrior, battle maid (English)

Bedelia: possesses strength (French); exalted one (Gaelic)

Beela: black cockatoo (Aboriginal)

Bel: apple tree (Hindi); beautiful (French)

Bela: bright (Hungarian); white (Slavic)

Belda: beautiful (French / Italian)

Belica: dedicated to God (Spanish)

Belina: beautiful woman (German); beautiful (Spanish)

Belinda: beautiful (Italian)

Bella: beautiful (Italian)

Belle: beautiful (French / Italian)

Bellanca: beautiful, fair haired, blonde (Greek)

Benah: wisdom (Hebrew)

Benita: blessed (Latin / Spanish)

Berdine: one who shines brightly from within (German)

Bernice: strong, warrior, victory bringer (Greek)

Bernadette: strong, little warrior (French); strong brave bear (German)

Bernadine: strong, little warrior (French); strong brave bear (German)

Bernia: warrior (Latin)

Berry: berry (English); white box tree (Aboriginal)

Bertha: bright, famous, shining (English)

Beryl: green jewel (Greek)

Bessie: God's promise (Hebrew)

Beth: from the house of God (Hebrew)

Betha: life (Celtic)

Bethanny: from the house of God's grace (Aramaic)

Bethel: house of God (Hebrew)

Bethesda: from the house of mercy (Hebrew)

Bethia: daughter of Jehovah (Hebrew); life (Gaelic)

Betsy: God's promise (Hebrew)

Bette: God is my oath (Hebrew)

Betty: God is my oath (Hebrew)

Betulah: women (Hebrew)

Beulah: bride (Hebrew)

Beverly: beaver stream or meadow (English)

Bian: secret (Vietnamese)

Bianca: white, pure (Italian)

Bibi: lady of the house (Persian)

Bibiana: alive, lively (Latin)

Bilhah: tender (Hebrew)

Billie: wilful (English); helmet, protection (German)

Bina: dancer (Swahili); knowledge, understanding (Hebrew)

Binda: deep water (Aboriginal)

Bjorg: help, salvation (Scandinavian)

Bladina: warm and friendly (Latin)

Blaine: flame (English); yellow (Gaelic)

Blair: field (Scottish)

Blaise: burning flames (English); stutter (Latin)

Blanca: white, blonde (Spanish)

Blanche: white, fair haired (French)

Blanda: gives compliments (Hebrew); seductive (Latin)

Bliss: bringer of happiness, joy (English)

Blossom: blooming flower (English)

Blythe: cheerful, gentle (English)

Boann: white cow (Irish)

Bobbi: bright, famous (German); foreign woman (Latin)

Bodil: warrior (Norse)

Bombala: where the waters meet (Aboriginal)

Bona: good (Latin)

Bondi: sound of tumbling water (Aboriginal)

Bonita: little, pretty (Spanish)

Bonne: good, attractive, pretty (Scottish)

Bonnie: good, attractive, pretty (Scottish)

Branda: blessing (Hebrew)

Brandy: brandy (Dutch)

Breana: gracious victory, strong (Celtic)

Bree: strong victory (Irish); from the boundary line (Latin)

Breen: from the fairy palace (Irish)

Brenda: fire stoker, mark by burning (English); sword (Norse)

Brieena: little raven, raven haired (Gaelic)

Bretta: from Britain (Gaelic)

Bria: hill, high, exalted (Gaelic); honorable, strong (Celtic)

Brianna: hill, graceful victory, honorable, exalted (Celtic)

Brianne: hill, graceful victory, honorable, exalted (Celtic)

Briar: heather (French); thorny bush (English)

Bridget: strength (Irish); exalted one (Gaelic)

Brie: from Brie in France, marshland (French)

Brielle: heroine of God (Hebrew)

Brina: boundary (Latin); honorable (Irish); defender (Slavic)

Brita: strong spirit (Irish); from Britain (English); exalted (Norwegian)

Britt: strong spirit (Irish); from Britain (English); exalted (Norwegian)

Britta: strong spirit (Irish); from Britain (English); exalted (Norwegian)

Brittany: from Britain (Irish)

Bronwyn: fair (Welsh)

Brooke: from the stream (English)

Bruna: armored warrior (German); brown skin (Italian)

Bryga: strength (Polish)

Bryn: boundary (Latin); from the mountain, hill (Welsh)

Bryony: cottage (German); twisting vine, climbing plant (English)

Buffy: polisher (English); buffalo of the plains (Native American)

Byanna: hill (Irish); honorable, strong (Celtic); near the graceful one (English)

Byhalia: white oak (Native American)

C

Cadence: beat, rhythm (Latin)

Caeley: crown of laurel leaves in the meadow (Hebrew); from the pure meadow (English)

Caera: brown or red complexion (Irish); dearly loved friend (Latin)

Cai: woman, feminine (Vietnamese)

Cailida: adorable (Spanish)

Cailin: from the pure pool (Welsh); girl (Gaelic)

Caitlin: from the pure pool, pure (Irish)

Cala: castle, fortress (Arabic)

Calamity: misfortune (Latin)

Calandra: carefree, lark bird, lovely one (Greek)

Calantha: flower, beautiful flower (Greek)

Calca: star (Aboriginal)

Caley: slim, fair (Irish)

Calida: ardent, most beautiful, warm (Spanish)

Calla: beautiful (Greek)

Callan: talkative (German); to cry out (Norse); rock (Scottish)

Callie: fortress (Arabic); beautiful (Greek)

Callista: beautiful (Greek)

Callula: small beauty (Latin)

Calumina: little dove (Scottish)

Calvina: bald (Latin)

Calypso: hidden, one who hides (Greek)

Cambria: from Wales (Latin); the people (Welsh)

Camelia: beautiful flower, helper to the priest (Latin)

Cami: messenger, young ceremonial attendant (French); crooked nose, helper to the priest (Latin)

Camilla: messenger, young ceremonial attendant (Latin / French)

Camille: messenger, young ceremonial attendant (Latin / French)

Canace: daughter of the wind god (Greek)

Candice: glowing, pure white (Greek); clarity (Latin)

Candra: glowing (Latin)

Candy: pure, white glow (Latin); confectionery, sweet (English)

Cantara: small crossing, bridge (Arabic)

Cantrelle: like a song (French)

Capri: fanciful (Italian)

Caprice: fanciful (Italian)

Cara: much loved (Italian)

Caress: soft touch, tender (French)

Carey: castle on the rocky island (Welsh); love (Gaelic)

Cari: gentle stream (Turkish); love (Gaelic)

Carina: little darling (Spanish); much loved (Latin)

Carissa: beloved (Greek)

Carita: charity, love (Latin)

Carla: free man (German); strong woman (English)

Carlene: free man (German)

Carlissa: free man (German)

Carlotta: little woman, courageous, strong (Italian); free man (German)

Carly: free man (German)

Carma: fruit field, orchard (Arabic); destiny (Sanskrit)

Carmela: garden, vineyard, orchard (Hebrew)

Carmen: song (Latin); garden, orchard (Hebrew)

Carmine: scarlet, red (Latin); garden, orchard (Hebrew)

Carna: horn (Latin)

Carnelian: red or yellow translucent gemstone (Latin)

Carol: free man, strong or courageous (German); Christmas carol (English)

Corolann: free man, strong or courageous (German); courageous, graceful, strong (English)

Carolina: free man, strong or courageous (German); joyful part of a Christmas song (English); little woman (Italian)

Caroline: free man, strong or courageous (German)

Caron: kind-hearted, loving (Welsh); pure (Greek)

Carpathia: fruit (Greek)

Carra: friend (Irish)

Carrie: little courageous woman (French); free man (German)

Caryl: beloved (Welsh); free man (German)

Caryn: purity (Danish)

Carys: love (Welsh)

Casey: brave (Irish); alert, watchful (Gaelic)

Cassie: prophet, shining upon man (Greek)

Cassandra: prophet, shining upon man (Greek)

Cassia: flowering (Latin); spice (Greek)

Cassidy: clever, curly hair (Irish)

Catherine: purity (Greek)

Cathleen: purity (Irish)

Cathy: purity (Greek)

Catrina: purity (Slavic)

Cayla: crown of laurel (Hebrew); slim and fair (Irish)

Ceara: this year (Gaelic); bright, famous (Latin)

Cecania: freedom (German)

Cecilia: blind (Latin)

Ceinlys: beautiful, sweet (Welsh)

Celandine: little swallow, yellow flowering plant (Greek)

Celena: heavenly, moon (Greek)

Celeste: heavenly, moon (Greek)

Celie: heavenly, moon (Greek)

Celine: heavenly, moon (Greek)

Cella: she is freedom (Italian)

Celosia: aflame, flaming (Greek)

Cera: red or brown complexion, cherry (Irish / Welsh)

Cerelia: springtime (Latin)

Cerella: springtime (Latin)

Ceres: goddess of the harvest (Roman)

Cerise: cherry (French)

Cerys: love (Welsh)

Chaanach: graceful, god has favored me (Hebrew)

Chablis: dry white wine (French)

Chadee: from Chad (French)

Chahna: loving (Hindi)

Chai: life (Hebrew)

Chaka: energy circle (Sanskrit)

Chakra: energy circle (Sanskrit)

Chalice: goblet, cup (French)

Chalonna: solitary (Latin)

Chamania: sunflower (Hebrew)

Chambrray: light fabric (French)

Chan: sweet smelling tree (Cambodian)

Chana: God is gracious, God has favored me (Hebrew)

Chanda: hot, passionate (Sanskrit)

Chandani: moonlight (Hindi)

Chandella: candle (French)

Chandra: moon (Sanskrit)

Chandria: moon (Sanskrit)

Chanel: from the straight, pipe (French)

Chanina: graceful (Hebrew)

Chantal: stone (French)

Chantelle: stone (French)

Chantara: song (American); stone (French)

Chantilly: fine lace (French)

Chara: joy (Greek); free man (German)

Charis: graceful (Greek); tender touch (French)

Charissa: graceful (Greek); tender touch (French)

Charisse: graceful (Greek); tender touch (French)

Charity: caring, charitable (Latin)

Charla: courageous, strong (English); free man (German)

Charleen: free man (German)

Charlie: free man (German)

Charlotte: little courageous woman (French); free man (German)

Charmaine: courageous, strong (German); charm (English)

Charo: little rose (Spanish); rosary (Latin)

Charrissee: cherry (French)

Chasca: goddess of the dawn (Incan)

Chastity: purity (Latin)

Chava: life, living (Hebrew)

Chavi: little girl (Gypsy)

Chavon: goddess gracious (Hebrew)

Chaya: life (Hebrew)

Chaylea: life meadow (English)

Cheera: happy (Greek)

Chelsea: from a chalk sea, from the port of ships (English)

Chemarin: girl who wears black (Hebrew)

Chen: precious (Chinese)

Chenetta: goose (Greek); oak tree (French)

Chenia: God is gracious (Hebrew)

Cher: dear (French)

Cherelle: dear, much loved (French)

Cherie: beloved cherry tree, dear (French)

Cherilyn: from the cherry tree near the pool (Welsh); dear (French)

Cherise: cherished, cherry (French)

Cherish: cherished, care for (English)

Cherry: much loved (French); cherry fruit (English)

Cheryl: cherry fruit, green gem (Welsh)

Cheyenne: graceful oak tree (French); speaker who you cannot understand (Native American)

Chezna: peace (Slovak)

Chiara: bright, famous (Italian)

Chika: much loved, near and dear (Japanese)

Chiku: one who chatters (Swahili)

Chilail: snowbird (Native American)

Chimene: hospitable (French)

Chiquita: little girl (Spanish)

Chita: kitten (Arabic); conception (Latin)

Chiyo: eternal, 1000 generations (Japanese)

Chloe: flowering, goddess of agriculture, green shoot (Greek)

Chloris: green, green-yellow (Greek)

Cho: beautiful (Korean); born at dawn, butterfly (Japanese)

Cholena: bird (Native American)

Chikri: blessed (Swahili)

Chrissanth: golden flower (French)

Chrissy: Christian (Latin)

Christa: Christian (Latin)

Christabel: beautiful Christian (Latin)

Christen: Christian (Latin)

Christian: Christian (Latin)

Christie: little Christian (Latin)

Christina: little Christian (Latin)

Christine: little Christian (French)

Christy: Christian (Latin)

Chrys: Christian (English)

Chrysanthe: golden flower (Greek)

Chryseis: golden daughter (Latin)

Chu: pearl (Chinese)

Chunami: dew drop (North American)

Ciana: light (Italian)

Ciannait: ancient (Irish)

Ciara: black (Irish)

Cicely: blind (Latin)

Cien: ancient (Irish)

Cindy: from Mount Kynthos (Greek)

Cinnia: curly haired (Latin)

Cipriana: lady from Cyprus (Italian)

Cirilla: lord (Greek)

Cissy: sister (English); blind (Welsh)

Claire: brilliant, famous (Latin)

Clara: brilliant, famous (Latin)

Clare: brilliant, famous (Latin)

Clarest: most brilliant (French)

Claribell: beautiful, bright, clear (Latin)

Clarice: fame (Latin)

Clarinda: bright, famous (Latin); brilliant, beautiful (Spanish)

Clarissa: bright, famous (Latin)

Clarita: bright, famous (Latin)

Claudette: little weak one (French)

Claudia: weak, lame (French)

Cleantha: glory flower (Greek)

Clementia: merciful (Latin)

Clementine: merciful (Latin)

Cleo: little fame (Greek)

Cleone: famous, glory (Greek)

Cleopatra: glory of the father (Greek)

Cleta: glory (Greek)

Clio: proclaimer, glory (Greek)

Clorinda: famous beauty (Persian)

Clove: aromatic spice, nail (Latin)

Clover: four leaf clover, luck, wealth (English)

Clymene: famous (Greek)

Coco: coconut (Spanish)

Colette: people of victory (French)

Colina: from the coal pool (English); peaceful dove, young child (Irish)

Colleen: girl (Irish)

Combara: tomorrow (Aboriginal)

Comfort: strengthen and comfort, comfort (English)

Concha: shell (Spanish); conception (Latin)

Conchetta: purity (Italian)

Conchita: the beginning (Spanish); conception (Latin)

Connie: constant (Latin)

Conradine: bold, wise counsel (German)

Constance: constant (Latin)

Consuela: consolation (Spanish)

Coolalie: south wind (Aboriginal)

Cora: girl, maiden (Greek)

Corabelle: beautiful girl (Greek)

Coral: from the sea (Latin)

Coralee: maiden (Greek)

Cordelia: jewel from the sea (Celtic); heart (Latin)

Cordella: warm hearted (Latin)

Coreita: girl (Greek)

Cori: girl (Greek)

Corina: girl (Greek)

Corinne: from the hollow (French); maiden (Greek)

Corisande: girl (Greek)

Corissa: girl (Greek)

Corliss: cheerful (English)

Cornelia: Cornell tree, horn colored (Latin)

Cornona: crowned (Latin)

Corra: from the mountain valley (Irish)

Cosette: lamb (German); little thing (French)

Cosima: universal harmony, order, beauty (Greek)

Courtney: of the court (English); short nosed (French)

Crystal: clear (Latin); gem, ice (Greek)

Cyrstalin: from the crystal pool (Welsh)

Curra: water spring (Aboriginal)

Cushla: dear, beat of my heart (Irish)

Cveta: flower (Slavic)

Cybil: prophet, mother of the gods (Greek)

Cyma: flowering, pregnant (Greek)

Cynara: artichoke, thistle (Greek)

Cynthia: moon (Greek)

Cyra: sun (Persian); lord (Greek)

Cryena: alluring one, siren (Greek)

Cyria: lordly ruler (Greek)

Cyriaca: child born on a Sunday (Greek)

Cyrilla: lordly ruler (Greek)

Czenzi: to increase (Hungarian)

D

Dacia: glowing, pure white (Greek)

Dae: born during the day (English)

Dahila: from the valley (Scandinavian)

Dahlia: dahlia flower, valley (English)

Dai: day (English); great (Japanese)

Daila: beautiful (Latvian)

Daisy: daisy flower, day's eve (English)

Daiya: gift (Polish)

Dakota: friend (North American)

Dale: from the valley (English)

Dalit: gentle, slender branch (Hebrew)

Dallas: from the dales or valley meadows (Irish)

Dalya: tree branch (Hebrew)

Dama: little noblewoman (Spanish)

Damaris: tame, gentle (Greek)

Damia: goddess of the forces of nature (Greek)

Damiana: tamed (Greek)

Damica: friendly (French)

Damita: little noblewoman (Spanish)

Dana: bright day, from Denmark (English)

Danessa: butterfly, God is my judge (Hebrew)

Daniah: God is my judge (Hebrew)

Danica: morning star (Slavic)

Danice: God is my judge (Hebrew)

Danielle: God is my judge (Hebrew)

Danna: God is my judge (Hebrew)

Dannal: God is my judge (Hebrew)

Dani: God is my judge (Hebrew)

Daphne: laurel tree (Greek)

Dara: compassionate, wisdom (Hebrew)

Darah: wisdom (Greek)

Daralis: beloved (English)

Darcelle: from the fortress, has dark hair (French); dark (Irish)

Darcy: dark haired, dark complexion (Irish)

Daria: wealthy (Greek)

Darice: queen (Persian)

Darielle: a gift (French); wealthy (Persian)

Darlilyn: little darling (English)

Darla: darling (English)

Darlene: darling (English)

Darnelle: she is darling (Irish); hidden nook (English)

Daron: great (Irish)

Darrelyn: beloved from the pool (English)

Daryl: gift (French)

Daryn: gift (Greek)

Dasha: gift of God (Russian)

Dashiki: African skirt (Swahili)

Davida: beloved (Hebrew)

Davita: beloved (Hebrew)

Davonna: beloved (Scottish)

Dawn: sunrise, dawn, daybreak, first light (English)

Daya: bird of prey (Hebrew); one with compassion (Sanskrit)

Dayna: bright day (English); from Denmark (English)

Dea: goddess (Latin)

Deana: divine (Latin); lives in the valley (English)

Deandra: brave, courageous one from the valley, strong (French); divine (Latin)

Deanna: divine, gracious (Latin); lives in the valley (English)

Debbie: bee (Hebrew)

Deborah: bee (Hebrew)

Debra: bee (Hebrew)

Dede: firstborn daughter (African); sorrowful (Welsh)

Dedra: sorrowful wander (Irish)

Dee-Dee: cherished (Hebrew)

Degula: excellent (Hebrew)

Deidre: sorrowful (Irish)

Deita: covering the earth, goddess of fertility (Greek)

Deja: before (French); remembrance (Spanish)

Deka: pleasing (Somalian)

Delana: noble protector (German)

Delany: the challenger's descendant (Irish); from the alder grove (French)

Deleena: little darling (French)

Delia: visible, from Delos (Greek)

Delicia: delightful, pleasure (English)

Dilija: sea daughter (Polish)

Delilah: one who broods (Hebrew)

Delma: from the sea (Spanish); noble protector (German)

Delores: sorrowful (Spanish)

Delphine: from Delphi, dolphin (Greek)

Deisie: sorrow (Spanish)

Delta: difference, fourth born daughter, fourth letter of the alphabet (Greek)

Delwyn: attractive, blessed (Welsh)

Delyth: attractive, neat (Welsh)

Demelda: to proclaim (Greek)

Demi: covering the earth, goddess of fertility (Greek); half (French)

Dena: valley (English)

Denae: innocent (Hebrew)

Deni: celebration, follower of Dionysius (French)

Denise: celebration, follower of Dionysius (French)

Denna: from the valley (English)

Deodata: God has given (Greek)

Derede: gift of God (Greek)

Derika: gifted ruler of the people (German)

Derora: stream (Greek); bird (Greek)

Deryn: bird (Welsh)

Desi: desired (French)

Desire: much desired (French)

Desiree: much desired (French)

Dessa: wandering (Greek)

Destiny: fate (French)

Deva: divine, goddess of the moon (Hindi)

Deveney: loved (Scottish); poet (Irish)

Devi: goddess of power and destruction (Hindi)

Dhara: from the earth (Hindi)

Diana: divine, graceful (English); goddess of the hunt, the moon, fertility (Latin)

Diane: divine, graceful (English); goddess of the hunt, the moon, fertility (Latin)

Diantha: divine flower (Greek)

Didi: beloved (Hebrew)

Dido: teacher (Greek)

Dilys: perfect, truth (Welsh)

Dima: raining (Hebrew)

Dinah: freedom, justified (Hebrew)

Dione: daughter of heaven and earth, mother of Aphrodite (Greek)

Dior: golden (French)

Dita: wealthy gift (Slavic)

Divinia: divine, heavenly (Latin)

Divya: divine, heavenly (Hindi)

Dixie: 10th born child, 10th (French); wall (English)

Diza: joy (Hebrew)

Doda: well loved (Hebrew)

Dodie: much loved (Hebrew)

Doli: blue bird (Native American)

Dolly: beautiful, doll like (English)

Dolores: sorrow (Spanish)

Domina: lady (Latin)

Dominica: lord (Latin)

Domino: lord (Latin)

Donata: gift, given (Latin)

Donna: lady (Italian)

Dora: gift (Greek)

Dorabella: beautiful gift (Greek)

Dore: golden (French); gift (Greek)

Doreen: moody, brooding (Irish); golden, gilded (French)

Dorena: golden girl (French); gift (Greek)

Doretta: little gift, gift from God (Greek)

Doria: gift (Greek)

Dorinda: beautiful gift (Greek)

Doris: gift (Greek)

Dorita: generation (Hebrew); gift of God (Greek)

Dorma: sleeping (Latin); home (Russian)

Dorothy: gift, gift of God (Greek)

Dorothea: gift, gift of God (Greek)

Dottie: gift (Greek)

Douna: from the valley (Slavic)

Dove: bird of peace (English)

Drina: helper of humankind (Spanish)

Druella: fast, level headed (Latin)

Drusilla: strength (Latin)

Dulcie: sweet (Latin)

Dustine: warrior (German)

Dyani: deer (Native American)

Dyllis: sincere, true (Welsh)

E

Eadda: prosperous (English)

Earlene: noble, princess, warrior (English)

Eavan: fair haired (Irish)

Ebba: flowing tide (English); brave (Norse)

Ebony: black, black wood (English)

Ebun: gift (Nigerian)

Eca: bird (Nigerian)

Echo: reflected sound (Greek)

Eda: happy (English)

Edana: desired (Celtic); little fiery one (Irish)

Edda: poetry, grandmother (Norse)

Eddi: property guardian (English); renewer (Hebrew)

Ede: generation (Greek); strive for wealth (English)

Edeline: noble, kind (German)

Eden: place of pleasure (Hebrew)

Edian: God's decoration (Hebrew)

Edina: prosperous, from Edinburgh (English)

Edith: happy, prosperous (English)

Ediva: wonderful gift (English)

Edlyn: small noble one, prosperous (English)

Edmee: wealthy protector (English)

Edna: wealthy protector (English); renewer (Hebrew)

Edrea: wealthy, powerful (English)

Edrice: strong property (English)

Edris: wealthy ruler (English); fiery leader, prophet (Welsh)

Edwina: wealthy friend (English)

Eepa: has supernatural powers (Hawaiian)

Effie: good reputation (Scottish); well spoken, pleasant (Greek)

Efia: born on Friday (African)

Efrata: respectable, fruitful, honored (Hebrew)

Efrona: sweet singing bird (Hebrew)

Ehani: desired (Hindi)

Eiddwen: fair, faithful (Welsh)

Eilah: oak, tree (Hebrew)

Eileen: shining light (Greek)

Eilwen: fair friend (Greek)

Eir: peaceful healer, goddess of medicine (Norse)

Eira: snow (Welsh)

Eiralys: snowdrop (Welsh)

Eirene: peaceful (Greek)

Eirian: silver (Welsh)

Eithne: fiery (Celtic); kernel (Irish)

Ekala: lake (Aboriginal)

Ela: noble, serene (Polish); tree, foreign (German)

Elaine: light, sunray (Greek)

Elama: people of God (Greek)

Elana: oak tree, tree (Hebrew); spirited (Slavic)

Elanora: from the seaside (Aboriginal)

Elata: elevated, praised, lofty (Latin)

Elrida: wise (English)

Eleanor: light, sunray (Greek)

Eleele: black eyes (Hawaiian)

Elena: shining light (Greek)

Eleni: shining light (Greek)

Elenola: bright (Hawaiian)

Eleora: God is my light (Greek)

Eletta: elf (English); footloose (Greek)

Elga: holy, sacred (Slavic)

Eli: light (Scandinavian); smart woman (Sanskrit)

Eliana: God has answered (Hebrew)

Elicia: noble (Hebrew)

Elidi: gift of the sun (Greek)

Elika: eternal ruler (Hawaiian)

Eliora: light of God (Greek)

Elisa: God's promise (Hebrew)

Elise: holy and sacred to God (French)

Elisha: noble, exalted (German)

Elissa: from the blessed isles (Greek)

Elita: chosen, special (Latin)

Eliza: holy and sacred to God (Hebrew)

Elizabeth: holy and sacred to God (Hebrew)

Elka: holy and sacred to God (Polish); noble (German)

Elke: noble (German)

Elle: she (French); sun ray, shining light (Greek)

Ellen: shining light (Scottish)

Elli: old soul (Norse); noble, exalted, shining light (German)

Ellice: noble, God is Lord (Greek)

Elma: fruit which is sweet (Turkish); helmet, protection (German)

Elmina: famous, noble (English); helmet, protection (German)

Elmira: princess (Arabic)

Elodie: flower, wealthy (Latin); marsh flower (Greek)

Eloisa: famous warrior (German)

Eloise: famous warrior (German)

Elsa: noble (German); God's promise (Hebrew)

Elsie: noble (German); God's promise (Hebrew)

Elva: white, noble, bright (Irish)

Elvina: little elf, magical being (English)

Elivira: blonde (Latin); closed (German); health (Spanish)

Elvie: elf (English); white, noble, bright (Irish)

Elvy: elf (English); white, noble, bright (Irish)

Elysia: blissful, sweet, home of the blessed (Latin)

Emmanuelle: God is with us (Hebrew)

Eme: loved (Hawaiian)

Emeni: amen (Tongan)

Emerald: green gemstone (French)

Emere: hard working (Maori)

Emily: hard working (German); rival (Latin)

Emma: hard working (German); rival (Latin)

Emmaline: peaceful home (French)

Emmylou: famous, hardworking warrior (German)

Ena: shining light (Irish); renewer (Hebrew)

Enakai: sea of fire (Hawaiian)

Endora: adorable, from the fountain of youth (Hebrew)

Enfys: rainbow (Welsh)

Engel: angel, messenger of God (Greek)

Engelina: angel, messenger of God (Greek)

Engracia: graceful (Spanish)

Enid: spirit of life (Welsh)

Enrica: ruler of the house (Spanish)

Enya: fiery, jewel (Scottish); kernel (Gaelic)

Epiphany: born on January 6 (Hebrew)

Epona: horse goddess (Roman)

Eponi: black, ebony (Tongan)

Erasma: desired (Greek)

Erela: angel (Hebrew)

Erica: brave ruler (English); ruler (Scandinavian)

Erin: from Ireland (Celtic); peace (Irish)

Erinna: from Ireland (Celtic); peace (Irish)

Eriline: little elf (English); promise (Celtic)

Eshe: life (Swahili)

Esi: born on Sunday (Ghanaian)

Esme: to love (French)

Esmeralda: emerald (Spanish)

Esperance: hope (French)

Estee: star (Persian)

Estelle: she is a star (French)

Esther: star (Persian)

Etenia: wealthy (Native American)

Ethana: reliable, steadfast, strong (Hebrew)

Ethel: noble (English)

Etoile: star, star like (French)

Etta: little (German)

Euganie: noble (Greek)

Eugaenia: noble (Greek)

Eulalia: well spoken (Greek)

Eunice: happy, good victory (Greek)

Eva: life (Hebrew)

Evaline: life (Hebrew)

Evangelina: angel, good news, messenger of God (Greek)

Evania: youthful warrior (Irish); peaceful (Greek)

Evanthe: flower (Greek)

Eve: life (Hebrew)

Eveleen: pleasant life (Celtic)

Evelyn: from the pool of life (Hebrew)

Evette: young archer (French)

Evita: life (Spanish)

Evonne: archer (French)

Ezra: helpful (Hebrew)

Ezrela: reaffirming the belief in God (Hebrew)

F

Fadila: purity, virtue (Arabic)

Fai: stingray (Tongan)

Faina: joyful (English)

Faine: joyful (English)

Fair: fair haired (English)

Fairlee: from the yellow meadow (English)

Faith: forever true (English)

Faizah: victorious (Arabic)

Falala: trustworthy (Tongan)

Falda: folding wings (Icelandic)

Faline: cat like (Latin)

Falzah: triumph (Arabic)

Faren: wandering, adventurous (English)

Farica: peacemaker, peaceful ruler (German)

Farrah: beautiful, pleasant, good looking (English); baby's nurse (Arabic)

Fatima: daughter of the prophet (Arabic)

Faustine: lucky (Latin)

Fawn: baby deer, fawn, reddish or brown hair (French)

Fay: fairy, true (French)

Fayme: famous reputation (French)

Fayre: fair hair (English)

Fayza: winner (Arabic)

Fealty: faithful (French)

Febe: bright, pure, shining (Italian)

Fedora: divine gift (Greek)

Feeli: fairy (Tongan)

Feena: little deer (Irish)

Feige: bird (Hebrew)

Felda: from the field (German)

Felice: fortunate (Greek)

Feiica: fortunate (Greek)

Felicity: fortunate, Roman goddess of good fortune (Latin)

Felise: happy, lucky (French)

Femi: love me (Nigerian); woman (French)

Fenna: fair hair (Norse)

Feronia: goddess of flowers (African)

Fiala: violet flower (Slavic)

Fidelity: faithful (Latin)

Fifi: God has added a child (French)

Filia: friend (Greek)

Filma: one who is veiled (German)

Filomena: she is loved (Greek)

Finna: fair haired (Irish)

Finola: fair haired, white shouldered (Gaelic)

Fiona: fair haired, ivory skin (Gaelic)

Fipe: bright (Polynesian)

Fira: fiery (English)

Fisi: flowering (Polynesian)

Flair: style (English)

Flame: fiery (Latin)

Flanna: fiery, red haired (Irish)

Flannery: fiery, red haired (Irish); flat metal (French)

Fleta: clean, beautiful, inlet of water (English); swift (German)

Fleur: flower (French)

Flora: flower (Latin)

Florence: flowering, in bloom (Latin)

Floria: blooming, flowering (Latin)

Florie: blooming, flowering (English)

Florine: blossoming flowers (Latin)

Floris: flowers (English)

Fola: honor (African)

Fontane: from the fountain (French)

Fontanna: from the fountain (French)

Fortuna: fortunate, lucky (Italian); good fate (Latin)

Fortune: fortunate, lucky (Italian); good fate (Latin)

Fosetta: dimple (French)

Fotini: light (Greek)

Fran: from France (Latin)

Francesca: French (Italian)

Franci: French (Latin)

Francine: French (French)

Frayda: joy (German)

Frazea: freedom (Spanish)

Freda: peaceful (German)

Frederica: peaceful ruler (German)

Frederique: peaceful ruler (German)

Freida: peaceful (German)

Freya: goddess of love, noble lady (Scandinavian)

Fronia: French (Latin)
Fusi: banana (Polynesian)
Fuyu: Winter (Japanese)

G

Gable: little one with strength of God (French)

Gabriella: strength of God (Italian); peaceful (German); heroine of God (Hebrew)

Gabrielle: strength of God (Italian); heroine of God (Hebrew)

Gaby: strength of God (Italian); heroine of God (Hebrew)

Gaetana: graceful Earth (Hebrew); from Gaeta (Italian)

Gai: lively, glad (French)

Gay: lively, glad (French)

Gaia: Earth (Greek)

Gail: born of a joyous father (Hebrew); lively singer (English)

Gala: fine (Italian); singer (Norwegian); festivity (French)

Galatea: cream colored (Greek)

Galaxy: star system (Latin)

Galena: calm heel (Greek)

Galilani: friend (North American)

Galina: calm (Greek); white light (Russian)

Galla: stranger (Celtic); festivity (Latin)

Gamel: elder (Scandinavian)

Ganesa: lucky (Hindi)

Ganya: garden of Lord (Hebrew)

Garda: guardian (German); shelter (Norse)

Garland: from the battleground (English); flower wreath (French)

Garyn: spear carrier (English)

Gasha: kind, good (Russian)

Gasparde: guardian of the treasure (French)

Gayadin: Platypus (Aboriginal)

Gaylia: lively (English)

Gayna: white and smooth (Welsh)

Gemma: gem, jewel (Latin)

Gena: well born, noble (Greek)

Geneva: juniper tree (French)

Genevieve: white (French)

Genna: white wave (Welsh)

Georgeanne: graceful farmer (Greek)

Georgene: farmer (English)

Georgette: little farmer (French)

Georgia: farmer (Latin)

Georgianna: graceful farmer (Latin)

Georgina: farmer (Latin)

Georginne: farmer (Latin)

Geraldine: brave spear carrier (German)

Geralyn: spear ruler (German)

Gerda: beloved warrior (German); shelter (Norse)

Geri: brave spear carrier (German)

Germaine: from Germany (French)

Germina: twin (Greek)

Gertrude: strong spear (German)

Gessica: wealthy (Italian)

Geva: hill (Hebrew)

Ghada: tender, young (Arabic)

Ghita: pearl (Italian)

Gia: God is gracious (Italian)

Giacitna: hyacinth, purple (Italian)

Gian: God is gracious (Hebrew)

Gidget: cute, giddy (English)

Gigi: brilliant (German)

Gila: joy (Hebrew)

Gilana: joy (Hebrew)

Gilda: covered in gold (English); God's servant (Celtic)

Gillian: young bird, youthful (Latin)

Gin: silver (Japanese)

Gina: farmer (Greek); garden (Hebrew); silver (Japanese)

Ginger: ginger spice, red haired (English)

Ginia: purity, maiden (Latin)

Ginnifer: fair haired, white wave (Welsh)

Ginny: purity, virgin (Latin)

Giordana: descending, following down (Italian)

Giovanna: God is gracious (Italian)

Gisa: carved stone (Hebrew)

Gisela: promise (German)

Giselle: protector with a sword (English); pledge, hostage (German)

Gita: pearl (Slavic); song (Sanskrit)

Gitana: gypsy (Spanish)

Githa: good (Greek)

Gladys: small sword, lame (Latin); princess (Celtic)

Glenda: from the valley (Irish); fair, good (Welsh)

Glenna: glenn, narrow valley between the hills (Irish)

Glennis: holy (Welsh)

Glynnis: holy (Welsh)

Gloria: glorious, glory (Latin)

Glorien: glorious (Latin)

Glory: glorious (Latin)

Godiva: gift of God (English)

Golda: gold (English)

Grace: blessed, graceful, favor (Latin)

Gracia: graceful, favor, blessing (Latin)

Gratiana: graceful (Hebrew); favor, blessing (Latin)

Greer: watchful (Scottish)

Greta: daisy (English); pearl (Greek)

Gretchen: pearl (German)

Gretel: pearl (Greek)

Grischa: watchful (Russian)

Griselda: war heroine, dark battle (German)

Guda: divine, good (Scandinavian)

Guilda: guide from the forest (Italian)

Guinevere: fair and smooth (Welsh)

Gunda: woman warrior (Norwegian)

Gwen: fair, white, blessed (Welsh)

Gwenda: fair, white, blessed (Welsh)

Gwendolyn: fair one from the pool (English); blessed ring (Welsh)

Gwyneth: happiness (Welsh)

Gypsy: wanderer (English)

H

Hadara: beauty, splendor (Hebrew)

Haidee: modest (Greek)

Haido: caress (Greek)

Hailey: hay meadow (English); hero (Scottish)

Haiwee: dove (Native American)

Hala: salty (Latin); halo Arabic)

Haldana: half Danish (Norse)

Haley: hay meadow, indigenous (English); heroine (Scandinavian)

Halia: she looks like a loved relative (Hawaiian)

Haliaka: house leader (Hawaiian)

Halima: gentle (Swahili)

Halimeda: one who thinks of the sea (Greek)

Halina: resemblance (Greek)

Halla: unexpected gift or guest (Swahili)

Hallie: one who thinks of the sea (Greek)

Halona: lucky (Native American)

Hana: blossom flower (Japanese); goddess gracious (Hebrew); work (Hawaiian)

Hanako: flower child (Japanese)

Hanele: merciful (Hebrew)

Hannah: God has favored me (Hebrew)

Hanya: stone (Aboriginal)

Hao: good, tasteful (Vietnamese)

Happi: delightful (English)

Harah: sky (Aboriginal)

Harlene: from the hare meadow (English)

Harley: from the hare meadow (English)

Harmony: harmonious (Latin)

Harriet: powerful army commander (French); home ruler (German)

Hasia: protected by the Lord (Hebrew)

Hasina: good, beautiful (Swahili)

Hateya: push away with the foot (Native American)

Haukea: snow (Hawaiian)

Hausu: bear yawning (Native American)

Hawa: rest of life (Hebrew); love (Arabic)

Haya: modest (Arabic); life (Hebrew)

Hayat: life (Arabic)

Hayley: high clearing, hay meadow (English)

Hazel: hazelnut tree, yellow brown color (English)

Healther: from the place where the heather grows (English)

Heavenly: angelic, heavenly (English)

Hebe: young (Greek)

Hedda: one who struggles (German)

Heidi: noble (Swiss); exalted nature (German)

Helen: shining light, sunray (Greek)

Helena: shining light, sunray (Greek)

Helga: holy (Norse)

Helki: to touch (North American)

Helma: protection (German)

Heloise: famous in war, healthy (French)

Helsa: swan (English); god's promise (Hebrew)

Henrietta: ruler of the house (French)

Hera: queen of the heavens, wife of Zeus (Greek)

Herma: square pillar made of stone (Latin); messenger, earthly (Greek)

Hermoine: daughter of the Earth, noble woman (Greek)

Hermosa: beautiful (Spanish); lovely (Latin)

Hestia: myrtle tree (Persian); goddess of the hearth (Greek)

Heta: hunting rabbits (North American)

Hialeah: beautiful meadow (North American)

Hika: daughter (Polynesian)

Hilary: cheerful (Greek)

Hilda: battle stronghold, warrior (German)

Hildemar: glorious (German)

Hilma: projected (German)

Hina: spider (Tongan)

Hinda: doe, female deer (Hebrew)

Hine: girl (Polynesian)

Hiriko: generous (Japanese)

Hisa: long-lived (Japanese)

Hiva: song (Tongan)

Hoaka: bright (Hawaiian)

Holla: goddess of fruitfulness (German)

Hollis: holly tree (English)

Holly: holly tree (English)

Honesta: honest, trustworthy (Latin)

Honey: honey, sweet (English)

Honor: honorable (Latin)

Hoolana: happy (Hawaiian)

Hope: desire, hope (English)

Hopi: peace (North American)

Horatia: promise (Greek); timekeeper (Latin)

Hoshi: star (Japanese)

Huata: seeds in the basket (North American)

Huelo: ray of light (Tongan)

Huette: heart, mind (German); intelligent (English)

Hula: maker of music (Hebrew)

Hunter: hunter (English)

Huyana: rain falling (Native American)

I

Ianira: enchantress (Greek)

Ianthe: violet colored, violet flower (Greek)

Ida: happy, hardworking, prosperous (English)

Idabelle: beautiful, happy, hardworking, prosperous (English)

Idalia: sun (Spanish)

Idelia: noble (German)

Idelle: bountiful, plenty (Celtic)

Idola: idolized, visionary (Greek)

Idra: fig tree (Aramaic)

Iesha: life (Swahili)

Ignacia: fiery, burning (Latin)

Ignia: fiery (Latin)

Ikia: God is my salvation (Hebrew)

Ila: island (French); light (Hungarian)

Ilana: tree (Hebrew)

Ilene: light (Irish)

Iliana: trojan (Greek); god has answered me (Hebrew)

Ilima: flower (Hawaiian)

Ilise: noble (German)

Ilisha: life (Hebrew)

Ilka: flattering (Scottish)

Ilona: beautiful, shining light (Hungarian)

Ilsa: noblewoman (German); god is my oath (Hebrew)

Ilysa: noble, exalted (Greek); logical (Greek)

Ima: hard-working, embracing everything (German); present (Japanese)

Imala: strong minded (North American)

Iman: believer (Arabic)

Imber: ginger (Polish)

Imelda: warrior, universal battle (German)

Imena: dreamer (African)

Imeria: royal (Latin)

Imogene: image, likeness (Latin); maiden, image of her mother (Irish)

Ina: purity (Irish)

Inari: lake (Finnish)

Inas: wife of the moon (Polynesian)

India: from India (Hindi)

Indiana: Indian territory (English)

Indigo: dark blue, violet (Latin)

Indira: great (Hindi)

Induna: hard-working (German); lover (Norse)

Inez: purity (Spanish)

Igna: beautiful daughter of the hero (Scandinavian)

Ingar: crayfish (Aboriginal)

Inge: extend (English); guarded by Ing (Norse)

Ingrid: beautiful daughter of the hero (Scandinavian)

Igiga: fiery (Latin)

Inoa: chanting (Hawaiian)

Inocencia: innocence, purity (Spanish)

Inola: black fox (North American)

Ioana: God is gracious, he has favored me (Hebrew)

Iola: violet colored flower (Greek); worthy of the Lord (Welsh)

Iolana: soaring like a hawk (Hawaiian)

Iolanda: purple, hyacinth (French); violet flower (Greek)

Ione: violet (Greek)

Iora: gold (Latin)

Ira: camp (Aboriginal); peace (Greek); watchful (Hebrew)

Irene: peaceful (Greek)

Iris: iris flower (English); rainbow (Greek)

Irma: complete (German); high ranking, noble (Latin)

Imrina: noble (Latin)

Irva: seafarer (English)

Irvette: little sea friend (English)

Isa: lady with the iron will (German); little (Greek); god's promise (Hebrew)

Isabella: dedicated to God (Spanish); god is my oath (Hebrew)

Isabelle: dedicated to God (Spanish); god is my oath (Hebrew)

Isadora: adored (English); gift of Isis (Latin)

Isatas: snow (North American)

Isha: woman (Hindi)

Isis: fertility, goddess of nature (Egyptian)

Isla: Ireland (Celtic)

Ismaela: God listens (Hebrew)

Ismena: wisdom (Greek)

Isoka: God's gift (Nigerian)

Isola: island (Italian)

Isolde: fair lady (Welsh); ruler (German)

Ita: thirsting for the truth (Gaelic)

Ituha: oak tree (Native American)

Iuana: wind over a bubbling stream (Native American)

Iva: willow (Russian); god is gracious (Hebrew)

Ivah: god is gracious (Hebrew)

Ivanna: god is gracious (Hebrew)

Ivory: ivory, white, creamy color (English)

Ivy: ivy vine (English)

Izusa: white stone (North American)

J

Jaamini: evening (Hindi)

Jacy: beautiful (Greek); purple (Spanish)

Jaci: replacer (Hebrew)

Jacinda: beautiful (Greek); replacer (Hebrew); purple (Spanish)

Jacinta: hyacinth, purple (Spanish)

Jacki: replacer (Hebrew)

Jacky: replacer (Hebrew)

Jacqui: replacer (Hebrew)

Jacqueena: replacer, replacer queen (Hebrew)

Jacqueline: replacer (French)

Jada: wisdom (Hebrew)

Jade: green gemstone (Spanish)

Jae: jay bird (Latin)

Jaehwa: beautiful (Korean)

Jael: wild mountain goat (Hebrew)

Jaha: dignified, proud (Swahili)

Jaia: victorious (Hindi)

Jaime: I love (French); one who supplants (Hebrew)

Jaimee: I love (French); one who supplants (Hebrew)

Jaira: God teaches (Hebrew)

Jakeisha: life (Swahili)

Jakinda: hyacinth, purple (Spanish)

Jala: clear (Arabic)

Jalena: God is gracious (Hebrew); temptress (Latin)

Jalila: great (Arabic)

Jalinda: pretty jay bird (Spanish)

Jalini: one who lives by the ocean (Hindi)

Jama: daughter (Sanskrit)

Jamelia: beautiful (Arabic)

Jami: replacer (Hebrew)

Jamie: replacer (Hebrew)

Jamila: beautiful, lovely (Arabic)

Jamilee: the meadow replacer (Hebrew)

Jamilynn: replacer from the pool (English)

Jan: God is gracious (English)

Jana: God is precious (Slavic)

Janae: God is gracious (Hebrew)

Janaia: fruit harvest (Arabic)

Janaki: mother (Hindi)

Janan: she has a heart and soul (Arabic)

Jane: God is gracious (Hebrew)

Janie: God is gracious (Hebrew)

Jayne: God is gracious (Hebrew)

Janel: God is gracious (Hebrew)

Janelle: God is gracious (Hebrew)

Janessa: God's precious butterfly (Hebrew)

Janet: God is gracious (Hebrew)

Jania: God's gracious gift (Hebrew)

Janice: God is gracious (Hebrew)

Janika: God is gracious (Hebrew)

Janine: God is gracious (Hebrew)

Janique: God is gracious (Hebrew)

Janita: God is gracious (Hebrew)

Janna: God is gracious (Hebrew); fruit harvest (Arabic)

Jannali: moon (Aboriginal)

Jany: fire (Hindi)

Japera: complete (Zimbabwean)

Jardena: descending, flowing down (Hebrew)

Jarita: legendary bird (Hindi); water jug (Arab)

Jarmilla: Spring (Slavic)

Jarnila: beautiful (Arabic)

Jasia: God is gracious (Hebrew)

Jasmina: fragrant flower, jasmine flower (Persian)

Jasmine: fragrant flower, jasmine flower (Persian)

Jassi: jasmine flower (Persian)

Jatara: God is gracious (Hebrew)

Javana: graceful one from Java (Malaysian)

Javiera: bright (Spanish)

Jay: blue crested bird (Latin)

Jaya: victorious (Hindi)

Jaylene: blue crested bird (Latin)

Jayna: God is gracious (Hebrew)

Jayne: God is gracious (Hebrew); victorious (Sanskrit)

Jazlyn: from the jasmine flowers near the pool (Persian)

Jean: God is gracious (Hebrew)

Jeanette: God is gracious (French)

Jedda: beautiful girl (Aboriginal)

Jelena: shining light (Russian)

Jemma: little gem (English)

Jemima: doves of peace (Hebrew)

Jemina: gem child of the Earth (Czech)

Jena: small bird (Arabic)

Jendaya: thankful (Zimbabwean)

Jenelia: from the white meadow (Welsh)

Jenelle: God is gracious (French); to give in (English)

Jenice: goddess gracious (Hebrew)

Jenilee: white wave from the meadow (Welsh)

Jenna: fair, white haired (Welsh)

Jennalyn: white wave in the pool (English); heaven (Arabic)

Jennica: God is gracious (English)

Jennifer: white wave, their haired (English); fair and smooth (Welsh)

Jenny: white (Welsh)

Jeraldine: brave spear carrier (German)

Jeremia: chosen by God (Hebrew)

Jereni: peaceful (Russian)

Jeri: brave spear carrier (German)

Jerica: mighty warrior ruler (German)

Jerilyn: brave spear carrier from the pool (German)

Jermaine: from Germany (French)

Jerusha: inheritance, marriage (Hebrew)

Jessalin: wealthy one from the pool (Hebrew)

Jessamine: jasmine flower, wealthy (French)

Jesse: wealthy (Hebrew)

Jessenia: flower (Arabic)

Jessica: wealthy, he sees (Hebrew)

Jessie: wealthy, he sees (Hebrew)

Jususa: God will help (Hebrew)

Jewel: precious gemstones (French)

Jewelana: precious or graceful gemstone (English)

Jezebel: beautiful, wealthy (Spanish); wicked (Hebrew)

Jiana: graceful (English)

Jill: youthful (Latin)

Jillaine: youthful (Latin)

Jilli: today (Aboriginal)

Jillian: youthful (Latin)

Jimena: hearing (Spanish)

Jin: tender (Japanese)

Jina: farmer (Greek); named child (Swahili)

Jinny: white wave (Welsh)

Jinx: spell (Latin)

Jirakee: cascade, small waterfalls (Aboriginal)

Jirina: farmer (Slavic)

Jivanta: creating (Hindi)

Jizelle: promise (German)

Jo: God is gracious (Hebrew)

Joakima: God will establish (Hebrew)

Joan: God is gracious (Hebrew)

Joanna: God is gracious and graceful (Hebrew)

Joanne: God is gracious and graceful (Hebrew)

Joaquina: God establishes (Hebrew)

Jobeth: from the house of gracious God (Hebrew)

Joby: afflicted, distressed (Hebrew)

Jocelyn: joyful (Latin); just (English)

Jodi: admired, praised, from Judea (Hebrew); playful (Latin)

Jodie: admired, praised, from Judea (Hebrew); playful (Latin)

Jody: admired, praised, from Judea (Hebrew); playful (Latin)

Johanna: God is gracious (Hebrew)

Joelle: God is willing (Hebrew)

Johnna: God is gracious (Hebrew)

Joia: happy, joy (French)

Jolan: violet flower (Hungarian)

Jolanda: hyacinth, purple (Greek)

Jolena: pretty (French)

Jolene: God increases (Hebrew)

Jolie: highly spirited (English); pretty (French)

Joline: God has added a child (Hebrew)

Jonelle: she is gracious to God (French)

Joni: God is a gracious (Hebrew)

Jonina: dove (Hebrew)

Jonita: happy (Latin); peace (Hebrew)

Jonna: God is gracious (English)

Jontel: God is gracious (Hebrew)

Jora: born during the autumn rain (Hebrew)

Jordan: descending, flowing down (Hebrew)

Jorja: farmer (Greek)

Josea: God will increase (French)

Josee: God will increase (French)

Josephine: God will increase (Hebrew)

Josetee: God has added a little child (French)

Josie: God has added a little child (French)

Jovanna: love (Latin)

Jovi: joyful (Latin)

Joy: joyful (Latin)

Joyanna: joyful grace (English)

Joyce: joyful (French)

Joyita: jewel (Spanish)

Joyln: archer from the pool (English)

Juana: God is gracious (Spanish)

Juanita: God is gracious (Spanish)

Judith: praised, from Judea (Hebrew)

Judy: praised, from Judea (Hebrew)

Jula: flower (Hindi)

Julene: youthful (Latin)

Julia: youthful (Latin)

Julie: youthful (Latin)

Juliana: youthful grace (Slavic)

Juliet: little youth (French)

June: born in June (Latin)

Junee: speaking (Aboriginal)

Juno: queen of the heavens (Latin)

Jurisa: storm (Slavic)

Justine: righteous (Latin)

Jyoti: light (Hindi)

K

Kachine: sacred dancer (Native American)

Kacie: alert (Irish)

Kadla: sweet (Aboriginal)

Kagami: reflection (Japanese)

Kahi: shellfish (Tongan)

Kai: forgive (Japanese); sea (Hawaiian); willow tree (Native American)

Kaila: call out (Tongan)

Kailani: sea, sky (Hawaiian)

Kailmana: diamond (Hawaiian)

Kaina: beautiful (Welsh); eastern sky (Hawaiian)

Kaisa: purity (Swedish)

Kaitlin: pure (Irish)

Kaiyo: one who is forgiven (Japanese)

Kahaka: glowing with heat (Tongan)

Kakala: sweet smelling flower (Tongan)

Kakalina: purity (Hawaiian)

Kakata: laughing (Tongan)

Kakra: second born twin (Ghanaian)

Kal: yellow flower (English)

Kala: black (Hindi); sun (Hawaiian)

Kalala: bright (Hawaiian)

Kalama: flame (Hawaiian)

Kalameli: caramel (Tongan)

Kalana: flat land (Tongan)

Kalani: sky (Hawaiian)

Kalasia: grace (Tongan)

Kalauka: famous (Hawaiian)

Kalauni: crown (Tongan)

Kalea: bright (Hawaiian)

Kalei: from the pure meadow (English); flower wreath (Hawaiian)

Kali: black (Sanskrit); one who hesitates (Hawaiian)

Kalia: double canoe (Tongan)

Kalika: rosebud (Greek)

Kalia: beloved (Arabic)

Kalina: flower (Polish)

Kalinda: view (Aboriginal); sun (Sanskrit)

Kalinn: river (Scandinavian)

Kaliope: beautiful (Greek)

Kalistala: crystal (Tongan)

Kaliska: coyote chasing deer (Native American)

Kalla: fiery (Aboriginal)

Kallista: beautiful (Greek)

Kallolee: happy (Hindi)

Kaloni: perfume (Tongan)

Kaloti: carrot (Tongan)

Kalou: crow (Tongan)

Kalyan: stay near (Aboriginal)

Kama: love (Sanskrit)

Kamala: lotus flower (Sanskrit)

Kamili: angel of newborn babies (Zimbabwean)

Kamaria: moon (African)

Kamata: fortune, fate (Native American)

Kamballa: young woman (Aboriginal)

Kame: turtle (Japanese)

Kamea: only child (Hawaiian)

Kameko: child who lives long (Japanese)

Kameli: honey (Hawaiian)

Kami: Lord (Japanese)

Kamilah: perfection (Arabic)

Kamilia: sweet flower (Slavic)

Kamille: perfection (Arabic)

Kamoana: ocean (Hawaiian)

Kanali: canal (Tongan)

Kanani: beautiful (Hawaiian)

Kanda: smile (Kurdish)

Kaneli: canary, yellow (Tongan)

Kani: sound (Hawaiian)

Kaniva: Milky Way galaxy (Tongan)

Kannitha: angel, messenger of God (Cambodian)

Kanya: purity (Hindi); young girl (Sanskrit)

Kaoru: perfume, strength (Japanese)

Kapika: gazelle (Hawaiian)

Kara: possum (Aboriginal); black (Turkish)

Karalana: like (Greek); possum (Aboriginal)

Karan: purity (Greek)

Karen: purity (Greek)

Kareela: wind of the South (Aboriginal)

Karenza: affectionate, loving (English)

Karida: purity (Greek); virgin (Arabic)

Karima: generous, noble (Arabic)

Karis: graceful (Greek)

Karisma: favorite gift (Greek)

Kariss: favorite (Greek)

Karissa: favorite (Greek)

Karla: free man (German)

Karli: covered in snow (Turkish)

Karma: destiny, fate (Sanskrit)

Karmel: fruitful vineyard, God's garden (Hebrew)

Karmiti: tree (African)

Karniela: horn (Hebrew)

Karol: free man (German)

Karolina: free man (German)

Karri: Eucalyptus tree (Aboriginal)

Karrin: evening time (Aboriginal)

Kasimira: peace is announced (Slavic)

Kasota: clear sky (Native American)

Kassandra: shining upon man (Greek)

Kassia: cassia tree (Hebrew); purity (Greek)

Kassidy: clever, curly head (Gaelic)

Kate: purity (Greek)

Kateri: purity (Native American)

Kath: purity (Greek)

Katherine: purity (Greek)

Kathleen: purity (Greek)

Katina: firstborn child (Aboriginal); little pure one (Greek)

Katriel: God is my crown (Aboriginal)

Katrina: purity (Scandinavian)

Katrinelle: she is purity (French)

Kawana: wild flower (Aboriginal)

Kay: purity (Greek)

Kaya: place of rest (Japanese)

Kayalana: pure light (Greek)

Kayla: crown (Hebrew); purity (English)

Kaylee: from the pure meadow (English); slender (Gaelic)

Kazimiera: peace is proclaimed (Polish)

Keala: pathway (Hawaiian)

Kedma: towards the east (Hebrew)

Keely: beautiful (Irish)

Keena: brave, fast (Irish)

Kefria: young lioness (Hebrew)

Kei: glorious (Hawaiian)

Keighlea: pure one from the meadow (Irish)

Keja: purity Swedish

Keiki: child (Hawaiian)

Keiko: adored, pretty (Japanese)

Keilana: glorious calm (Hawaiian)

Keilani: glorious chief (Hawaiian)

Keina: moon (Aboriginal)

Keisha: favorite (Swahili)

Kelby: well by the place near the fountain spring (Scandinavian); farmhouse near the stream (English)

Kelda: clear mountain, spring of life (Scandinavian)

Kele: clay (Tongan)

Kelesi: grace (Tongan)

Keli: mine (Tongan)

Kelila: crown of laurel, victory (Hebrew)

Kelly: warrior, war (Irish)

Kelsey: victorious ship (English)

Kenda: greatest champion (Welsh)

Kendellana: chief of the valley of light (Greek)

Kendelle: chief of the valley (Celtic)

Kendra: knowledge (English); greatest champion (Welsh)

Kenisha: beautiful (English)

Kenna: knowledgeable (English)

Keohi: woman (Hawaiian)

Kerani: sacred bells (Hindi)

Keren: animal horn, ray of light (Hebrew)

Kerensa: affection, love (English)

Kerenza: like (Hebrew)

Kereru: pigeon (Polynesian)

Kerrianne: dark haired graceful one, black (Celtic)

Kerrielle: she who is dark (Celtic)

Kerry: dark haired (Celtic)

Keshet: rainbow (Hebrew)

Keshisha: elder (Arabic)

Kesi: daughter whose father is difficult (Swahili)

Kesia: favorite(African)

Ketina: girl (Hebrew)

Ketzia: cinnamon spice (Hebrew)

Keverne: handsome (Gaelic)

Kewanee: prairie hen (Native American)

Kezia: cassia tree, cinnamon spice (Hebrew)

Kia: beginning of the season (African)

Kiannah: God is gracious (Hebrew)

Kichi: fortunate (Japanese)

Kiki: castor plant Egyptian

Kiku: chrysanthemum flower (Japanese)

Kilia: heaven (Hawaiian)

Kilkie: water hen (Aboriginal)

Killara: one who is always there (Aboriginal)

Kim: royal (English)

Kimalina: chief who is noble and kind (Latin)

Kimana: butterfly (Native American)

Kimanna: chief whose God is gracious (Hebrew)

Kimberly: from the royal meadow (English)

Kimi: the best (Japanese)

Kimiko: heavenly, righteous child (Japanese)

Kimimela: butterfly (North American)

Kina: China (North American)

Kineta: active, alert (Greek)

Kinta: either (North American); laughing (Aboriginal)

Kioko: child born in happiness (Japanese)

Kiona: brown hills (Native American)

Kiowa: brown hills (Native American)

Kira: fireplace (Aboriginal); lady (Russian)

Kiran: ray of light (Hindi)

Kiri: tree bark (Maori)

Kirianne: God is gracious (Hebrew); tree bark (Maori)

Kirilina: tree bark by the pool of water (Maori)

Kirra: magpie (Aboriginal)

Kirsten: anointed, covered in oil (Scottish); follower of Christ (Latin)

Kirstie: anointed, covered in oil (Scottish); follower of Christ (Latin)

Kisa: kitten (Russian)

Kishi: brings happiness to the earth (Japanese)

Kissa: born after twins (Ugandan)

Kiva: protected (Hebrew)

Kiyoka: clear (Japanese)

Koana: God is good (Hawaiian)

Kodi: helpful (Irish)

Koemi: smiling a little (Japanese)

Kogarah: place where rushes grow (Aboriginal)

Kohia: passion flower (Polynesian)

Koko: night (Native American); stork (Japanese)

Koleyn: Winter (Aboriginal)

Kolina: young girl (Swedish)

Koloa: treasure (Tongan)

Kololia: glory (Tongan)

Kolora: lake (Aboriginal)

Kooanna: pure one whose God is gracious (Greek)

Koora: plenty (Aboriginal)

Kora: friend (Aboriginal); girl (Greek)

Korena: young girl, maiden (Greek)

Kornina: girl (English)

Kortanya: young fairy queen (Russian)

Kortina: young girl (Greek)

Koula: gold (Tongan)

Krisandra: prophet (Greek)

Kristen: Christian (Scandinavian)

Kristianna: Christian (Hebrew)

Kristine: Christian (Danish)

Krita: perfection (Sanskrit)

Krystal: clear (Latin); ice (Greek)

Kui: grandmother (Tongan)

Kuini: queen (Tongan)

Kula: bird (Tongan)

Kulya: pine nuts burning (Native American)

Kumala: sweet potato (Tongan)

Kumari: woman (Sanskrit)

Kumi: braid (Japanese)

Kumana: snow (Aboriginal)

Kuri: chestnut (Japanese)

Kyle: narrow, straight (Irish)

Kylie: boomerang (Aboriginal); from the meadow strait (Irish)

Kyna: intelligent, wise (Irish)

Kyoko: mirror (Japanese)

Kyra: sun (Persian)

Kyrene: lordly (Greek)

Kyrie: dark haired (Irish)

L

Lacey: delicate fabric (English)

Lachandra: moon (Sanskrit)

Lachianina: from the land of lakes (Scottish)

Lada: goddess of beauty (Russian); glorious ruler (Slavic)

Ladana: the mother of the gods (Finnish)

Ladancia: the morning star (French)

Ladasha: gift of God (Russian)

Ladawna: dawning (English)

Ladivina: divine (English)

Ladonna: lady (Italian)

Laella: elf (French)

Laetitia: happy (Latin)

Lahela: female deer (Hawaiian)

Laikana: Lila (Tongan)

Laili: dark haired (Arabic)

Laime: lime (Tongan)

Laine: light (English); wool (French)

Lainey: light (English); wool (French)

Laione: lion (Tongan)

Lais: happy (Greek)

Lajessica: wealthy (Hebrew)

Lajila: shy (Hindi)

Lajoia: happy (Latin)

Lajuanna: God is gracious (Hebrew)

Lajuliette: little youthful one (Latin)

Laka: alluring, siren (Hawaiian)

Lakalka: ballet dancer (Tongan)

Lakeisha: life (Swahili); woman (Arab)

Lakendra: understanding (English); greatest champion (Welsh)

Lakenya: jewel (African)

Laketa: the woods (Scottish)

Lakia: treasure (Arabic)

Lakkari: honeysuckle tree (Aboriginal)

Lakresha: rich reward (Latin)

Lakya: born on Thursday (Hindi)

Lala: tulip flower (Slavic)

Lalaka: walk (Tongan)

Lalasa: love (Hindi)

Lali: highest point of heaven (Spanish); wooden drum (Tongan); well spoken (Greek)

Lalirra: talkative (Aboriginal)

Lalita: charming, playful, honest (Sanskrit); talkative (Greek)

Lallie: talk (English)

Lamani: lemon (Tongan)

Lamesha: born under the sign of Aries (Hindi)

Lami: concealer (Tongan)

Lamia: bright land (German)

Lamis: softness (Arabic)

Lamora: honor (French)

Lamorna: the morning (English); beloved (French)

Lamya: dark lipped (Arabic)

Lana: light and airy (Hawaiian); woolly (Latin)

Landa: star of the sea, wished for (Hebrew)

Lane: narrow lane or little road (English)

Laneisha: life (Swahili); woman (Arab)

Lanelle: from the little road (French)

Lanet: little graceful one (Celtic); idol (Welsh)

Lani: heaven, sky (Hawaiian)

Lanni: light and airy (Hawaiian); woolly (Latin)

Lantha: purple flower (Greek)

Laquinta: the queen (English)

Lara: happy (Greek); famous (Latin)

Laraina: crown of laurel in the rain (English); famous warrior (Greek); sorrowful (Latin)

Laraine: crown of laurel in the rain (English); famous warrior (Greek); sorrowful (Latin)

Larana: seabird (Latin)

Lareina: queen (Spanish)

Lari: victory, holy (Latin)

Lariana: graceful, holy (Latin)

Laricia: holy crown of laurel leaves (Latin)

Lariel: lioness of God (Hebrew)

Larina: protection (Latin)

Larine: protection (Latin)

Larissa: happy (Greek)

Larlene: promise (Celtic)

Larmina: blue sky (Persian); born under the sign of Pisces (Hindi); love (German)

Larnelle: of high degree (Latin)

Lashanda: goodness gracious (Hebrew)

Lashawna: goodness gracious (Irish)

Lashonda: goodness gracious (Irish)

Lassie: little girl (Gaelic)

Lata: beautiful vine (Hindi)

Latara: rocky hill (Irish)

Latasha: born on Christmas day (Latin); birthday (American)

Lateefa: caress, gentle (Arabic)

Latia: joy (Latin)

Latika: little one (French)

Latisha: happy (Latin)

Latonia: goddess who gave birth to Diana and Apollo (Latin)

Latoya: victory, victorious one (Spanish)

Laulani: heavenly branch (Hawaiian)

Launoa: shining moon (Tongan)

Laura: laurel leaves (Latin)

Laurel: laurel leaves (Latin)

Lauren: laurel leaves (Latin)

Lavani: necklace (Tongan)

Laveda: purity (Latin)

Lavelle: she is purity (French); cleansed (Latin)

Laveni: lavender shrub, light purple color (Tongan)

Lavenita: lavender scent (Tongan)

Lavina: purity (Latin)

Lavinia: purity (Latin)

Lavonna: young archer (French)

Lawan: pretty (Thai)

Lawanda: wanderer (German)

Layla: child born during the night (Swahili); night beauty

(Arabic)

Leila: child born during the night (Swahili); night beauty (Arabic)

Layna: light (Greek)

Lea: lioness (Latin); meadow (English); tired (Hebrew)

Leah: lioness (Latin); meadow (English); tired (Hebrew)

Leigh: lioness (Latin); meadow (English); tired (Hebrew)

Leakiki: ocean waves (Polynesian)

Leala: faithful, loyal (French)

Leandra: faithful, like a lioness, loyal (Latin)

Leanna: bounded, legal (French); lioness (Latin)

Leanne: bounded, legal (French); lioness (Latin)

Leanore: compassion, light (Greek)

Lece: happy (French)

Lecia: happy (Latin)

Leda: happiness, lady (Greek)

Leeba: beloved one from the meadow (Yiddish)

Leena: water possum (Aboriginal)

Leeza: sacred, God's promise (Hebrew)

Legana: sea (Aboriginal)

Lehua: sacred (Hawaiian)

Leiko: arrogant (Japanese)

Leilani: child of heavenly flowers (Hawaiian)

Leire: bitter, star of the sea, wished for (Hebrew)

Leise: lace (Polynesian)

Lekasha: life (Swahili); woman (Arabic)

Lekeleka: of the moon (Tongan)

Lelei: wonderful (Tongan)

Leli: from the high tower (Swiss)

Lelia: fair speech (Greek)

Lelya: shining light (Russian)

Lemana: she oak tree (Aboriginal)

Lemula: devoted to God (Greek)

Lena: shining light (Latin)

Lenci: shining light (Hungarian)

Lene: shining light (German); soft, silky (Latin)

Leneisha: life (Swahili); woman (Arabic)

Leni: shining light (Latin)

Lenia: like a lioness (German)

Lenice: bold, strong like a lioness (German); soft, silky (Latin)

Lenis: smooth, soft (Latin)

Lenita: smooth, soft (Latin)

Lenore: shining light (Greek)

Leoda: woman of the people (Greek)

Leola: lioness (Latin)

Leolina: lioness (Welsh)

Leoma: bright light (English)

Leona: lioness (French)

Leonie: lioness like (French)

Lenora: shining light (Italian)

Leotina: like a lioness (Latin)

Leora: shining light (Hebrew)

Leota: woman of the people (German)

Leotie: prairie flower (Native American)

Lepati: leopard (Tongan)

Lera: breeze, healthy, strong (Russian); from the valley (English)

Lesi: pawpaw (Tongan)

Leslie: holly garden (Gaelic)

Leta: happy (Latin)

Letha: forgetful (Greek)

Leticia: happiness (Latin)

Leftifa: gentle (Arabic)

Letisha: happiness, joy (Latin)

Letitia: happiness (Latin)

Letricia: noble (Latin)

Letty: little strong courageous woman, happiness, joy (English)

Leura: lava (Aboriginal)

Levana: rising sun (Latin); white sun like the moon (Hebrew)

Levani: anointed with oil (Fijian)

Levania: morning sun, to rise (Latin)

Leveni: raven (Tongan)

Levia: attached, lioness of God (Hebrew)

Levina: lightning (English)

Levona: spice, incense (Hebrew)

Lewanna: moon, white (Hebrew)

Lexadra: defender of humankind (Greek)

Leya: law, loyalty (Spanish)

Lia: dependent (Hebrew); she brings good news (Greek)

Libby: sacred, holy to God (Hebrew)

Liberty: freedom (Latin)

Libusa: darling (Slavic)

Licha: noble (Spanish)

Lida: loved by the people (Slavic)

Lide: life (Latin)

Lidia: beautiful girl (Greek)

Lien: lotus flower (Chinese)

Liese: sacred, holy to God (German); god is my oath (Hebrew)

Liesha: life (Swahili); woman (Arabic)

Liesl: sacred, holy God (German)

Lila: unpredictable destiny (Hindi)

Lilac: lilac flower, light purple colored flower (English)

Lile: lily (Tongan)

Lilia: lily (Hawaiian)

Lilibeth: lily flower, sacred and holly to God (English)

Liliko: bird (Tongan)

Lilipilli: myrtle tree (Aboriginal)

Lilis: spirit of the night (Hebrew)

Lilith: belonging to the night (Arabic); lily (Latin); serpent (Hebrew)

Lillian: lily (Latin)

Lilo: generous, kind (Hawaiian); lily (Latin)

Liluye: chicken hawk (Native American)

Lily: lily flower, purity, innocence (Latin)

Lilybelle: beautiful lily (English)

Lin: beautiful jade stone (Chinese)

Lina: light (Italian)

Linda: beautiful, pretty (Spanish)

Lindel: from the open valley pool (English)

Lindie: beautiful, pretty (Spanish)

Lindsay: waterside, Lincoln's marsh (English)

Lindy: linden tree (English); serpent (German)

Linette: graceful, little (Celtic)

Linleigh: from the pool in the meadow (English)

Linnea: flower (Swedish)

Liolya: shining light (Russian)

Liona: lioness (Latin)

Lionetta: little lioness (Latin)

Liora: light (Hebrew)

Lira: river (Aboriginal)

Lirit: lyre music (Greek)

Liron: the song is mine (Hebrew)

Lirra: wren (Aboriginal)

Lis: lily (French)

Lisa: honeybee, holy and sacred to God (Greek)

Lisha: darkness before midnight (Arabic)

Lisle: from the island (English)

Liss: from the court (Celtic)

Lissa: honeybee (Greek)

Lissilma: there (Native American)

Lita: strong woman (Spanish)

Litonya: darting hummingbird (Native American)

Liv: olive (Latin); defense (Norse)

Livana: graceful olive (Latin); white like the moon (Hebrew)

Livia: joining (Hebrew); olive tree (Latin)

Liviya: brave lioness, crown (Hebrew)

Livona: spice (Hebrew)

Liz: holy, sacred god (English)

Liza: holy, sacred god (English)

Lizabeth: holy, sacred to God (English)

Lizina: holy, sacred to God (English)

Llawella: leader, lioness (Welsh)

Llian: linen (Welsh)

Loila: sky (Aboriginal)

Lois: famous warrior, superior (Greek)

Lola: strong woman, sorrows (Spanish)

Lole: attractive, candy (Tongan)

Lolita: sorrow (Spanish)

Lolotea: gift (Spanish)

Lomasi: pretty flower (North American)

Lona: solitary (Latin)

Lone: solitary (Latin)

Loni: lioness (Latin); solitary (English)

Lopeka: brightness, famous (Hawaiian)

Lopini: robin bird (Tongan)

Lora: delivering, siren, wine, crown of laurel leaves, victory (Latin)

Loree: delivering, siren, wine, crown of laurel leaves, victory (Latin)

Lorelei: delivering, siren, wine, crown of laurel leaves, victory (Latin)

Loren: crown of laurel leaves, victory (Latin)

Lorena: crown of laurel leaves, victory (Latin)

Lorenza: crown of laurel leaves, victory (English)

Loret: laurel (Latin)

Loretta: laurel (Latin)

Lori: alluring one, siren (German); crown of laurel leaves, victory (Latin)

Loriann: alluring one, graceful, graceful siren (English)

Loric: armor (Latin)

Lorice: crown of laurel leaves, victory (Latin)

Loricia: holy, crown of laurel leaves, victory (Greek)

Lorielle: she has a crown of laurel leaves (Latin); she is the alluring one, siren (French)

Lorina: crown of laurel leaves, victory (Latin)

Lorina: crown of laurel leaves, victory (Latin)

Loris: crown of laurel leaves, victory (Spanish)

Lorissa: crown of laurel leaves, victory (Latin)

Lorna: crown of laurel leaves, victory (Latin); lost love (English)

Lorraine: crown of laurel leaves in the rain (English); famous warrior (German)

Lorrelle: little crown of laurel leaves, little victory (French); she is victory (English)

Losa: rose (Polynesian)

Losaki: meeting (Polynesian)

Lotta: woman Swedish free man (German)

Lotte: little strong courageous woman (French); free man (German)

Lotus: dreamer, lotus flower (Greek)

Lou: famous warrior (German); leaf (Tongan)

Louam: sleep well (Ethiopian)

Louisa: famous warrior (German)

Louise: famous warrior (German)

Lourie: bird with bright feathers (African)

Lovai: heavy rain (Tongan); she is loved (English)

Lovinia: pure (Latin)

Lovisa: loved (English)

Luana: graceful warrior (Hebrew)

Luca: bringer of light (Italian)

Lucia: bringer of light (Latin)

Lucille: bringer of light (English)

Lucinda: bringer of light (Latin)

Lucindee: bringer of light (Latin)

Lucine: moon (Arabic)

Lucita: rewards, riches (Latin)

Lucy: light (Latin)

Ludella: clever, renowned (English)

Ludmilla: loved by the people (Slavic)

Luella: famous (English)

Luisa: famous warrior (Spanish)

Lulani: highest point of having (Maori)

Lulie: sleepy (English)

Lulu: owl (Tongan); pearl (Arabic)

Luna: moon (Latin)

Lundy: idle (Welsh); marsh (Gaelic)

Lunetta: little moon (Latin)

Luraline: alluring one, siren (German)

Lurline: alluring one, siren (German)

Lusa: holy, sacred to God (Finnish)

Luvena: little loved one (Latin)

Luyu: pecking bird (Native American)

Lyla: from the island (French)

Lynda: pretty (Spanish)

Linda: pretty (Spanish)

Lynette: idol (Welsh); uncertain (French)

Lynn: pool, lake, waterfall (English)

Lyonella: young lioness (French)

Lyris: player of the harp (Greek)

Lysandra: defender of human kind, freedom (Greek)

Lyzabeth: holy and sacred to God (Hebrew)

M

Mabel: worthy of love (Latin)

Macalla: full moon (Aboriginal)

Macria: happy (Greek)

Macawi: motherly, generous (Native American)

Macha: plain (Irish)

Macia: bitter (Polish)

Maciko: beautiful child (Japanese)

Mackenna: child of the handsome one (Gaelic)

Mada: from Magdalen, maiden, young unmarried woman (Hebrew); from the high tower (Greek)

Maddie: from Magdalen, maiden, young unmarried woman (Hebrew); from the high tower (Greek)

Madeleine: from Magdalen, maiden, young unmarried woman (Hebrew); from the high tower (Greek)

Madge: from Magdalen, maiden, young unmarried woman (Hebrew); from the high tower (Greek)

Madira: goddess of wine (Sanskrit)

Madison: son of mighty warrior (English)

Maeko: truthful child (Japanese)

Maeve: delicate, purple color (Gaelic); joy (Celtic)

Magena: the coming moon (North American)

Maggie: pearl (Greek)

Magnolia: magnolia tree blossom (Latin)

Mahal: love (Filipino)

Mahala: barren (Hebrew); woman of power (Native American)

Mahalia: affectionate, tender (Hebrew)

Mahesa: great lord (Hindi)

Mahila: woman (Sanskrit)

Mahina: moonlight (Hawaiian)

Mahira: energy (Hebrew)

Mahla: polished, one who shines (Hebrew); woman (Native American)

Mahola: dancing (Hebrew)

Maia: goddess of spring, right star, mother (Greek); woman (English)

Maida: woman (English)

Maimi: smile of truth (Japanese)

Maire: wished for, star of the sea, bitter (Irish)

Mairi: wished for, star of the sea, bitter (Hebrew)

Maisie: maize, sweetcorn (French)

Maita: lady of Zorro (Aramaic)

Maja: delightful, splendid (Arabic); great, mother (Greek)

Majid: delightful (Arabic); great, mother (Greek)

Makala: myrtle tree (Hawaiian)

Makana: gift (Hawaiian)

Makani: wind (Hawaiian)

Makara: child born under the sign of Capricorn (Hindi)

Makayla: child of purity (Greek)

Malana: light (Hawaiian)

Malania: dark haired (Greek)

Malaya: freedom (Filipino)

Malha: queen (Hebrew)

Mali: jasmine flower (Thai)

Malia: perhaps, probably (Hawaiian)

Maliaka: perhaps, probably (Hawaiian)

Malie: sweet (Tongan)

Malika: hard-working (Hungarian)

Malina: highly praised (Hebrew); peace (Hawaiian)

Malinda: gentle (Greek); sweet (Latin)

Malini: gardener, god of the Earth (Hindi)

Malka: queen (Arabic)

Malohi: strength (Tongan)

Malu: peacefulness (Hawaiian)

Malulani: under the skies of peace (Hawaiian)

Malva: mallow flower (Latin); tender (Greek)

Malvina: sweet friend, assistant (Latin); smooth brow (Gaelic)

Mana: miracle (Tongan); sensitive (Japanese)

Manda: warrior (Spanish)

Mandara: calm (Hindi)

Mandy: worthy of love (Latin)

Manette: little wished for, star of the sea, bitter (Latin)

Mangena: melody (Hebrew)

Mani: prayer (Chinese)

Manka: little wished for, star of the sea, bitter (Polish)

Manon: little wished for, star of the sea, bitter (French)

Mansi: picked flower (Native American)

Manuela: God is with us (Spanish)

Manya: wished for, star of the sea, bitter (Russian)

Mapiya: heaven (Native American)

Mara: black duck (Aboriginal)

Marabel: wished for, star of the sea, bitter (English)

Marah: melody (Hebrew)

Marcaria: happy (Greek)

Marcella: warrior, warlike, dedicated to Mars (Latin)

Marcena: warrior, warlike, dedicated to Mars (Latin)

Marcia: warrior, warlike, dedicated to Mars (Latin)

Marcie: warrior, warlike, dedicated to Mars (Latin)

Mardi: child born on Tuesday (French)

Maren: sea (Latin)

Maretta: pearl (Greek)

Marfa: wished for, star of the sea, bitter (Latin)

Margie: pearl (Greek)

Margaret: pearl (Greek)

Margo: pearl (Greek)

Marguerite: pearl (French)

Mari: ball (Japanese)

Maria: pearl (Hebrew)

Marie: pearl (Hebrew)

Mariah: God is my teacher (Hebrew)

Marian: wished for, star of the sea (Hebrew)

Mariana: wished for, star of the sea (Hebrew)

Maribella: wished for, star of the sea (English)

Marice: marsh flower (German); star of the sea (English)

Mariel: wished for, star of the sea (Dutch)

Markia: wished for, star of the sea (Dutch)

Mariko: circle (Japanese)

Marilla: wished for, star of the sea (Hebrew)

Marilyn: wished for, star of the sea, from the star of the sea pool (Hebrew)

Marina: of the sea (Latin)

Marini: healthy, pretty (Swahili)

Maris: from the sea, dark haired, from the moor (Latin)

Marion: wished for, star of the sea (Hebrew)

Marita: lady (Aramaic); sea (Spanish)

Maritza: blessed (Arabic)

Marja: wished for, star of the sea, bitter (Finnish)

Marjan: coral (Persian); wished for, star of the sea, bitter (Polish)

Marjolaine: marjoram, a sweet smelling plant (French)

Marjorie: pearl (Scottish)

Markeisha: warrior, warlike (Swahili)

Markie: warrior, warlike (Swahili)

Markita: pearl (Slavic)

Marla: wished for (Hebrew)

Marlee: wished for (Hebrew)

Marlene: praised highly (Hebrew)

Marlis: sacred, holy to God (Hebrew)

Marmara: shining (Greek)

Marmion: small (French)

Marney: happy Israeli sparkling, shining (Greek)

Marnina: happy Israeli sparkling, shining (Greek)

Maroula: wished for, star of the sea, bitter (Greek)

Marquise: noble (French)

Marquita: canopy (French)

Marree: place of possums (Aboriginal)

Marsala: an (Italian); town (Italian)

Marta: lady of sorrow (English)

Martha: lady (Aramaic)

Martina: warrior, warlike (Latin)

Martiza: blessed (Arabic)

Maru: gentle Polynesian round (Japanese)

Maruca: wished for, star of the sea, bitter (Spanish)

Marushka: wished for, star of the sea, bitter (Spanish)

Marvina: famous friend (French)

Mary: star of the sea (Latin)

Maryanne: star of the sea (Latin)

Marybeth: star of the sea (Latin)

Maryellen: star of the sea (Latin)

Maryjo: star of the sea (Latin)

Marylou: star of the sea (Latin)

Masada: foundation of strength (Hebrew)

Masani: one with the gap in her tooth (Swahili)

Mashika: child born during the rainy season (Swahili)

Matilda: strong powerful warrior, mighty in battle (German)

Matrika: mother (Sanskrit)

Matsuko: pine tree child (Japanese)

Mattea: gift of God (Hebrew)

Maud: strong powerful warrior (French)

Mauli: someone from New Zealand (Maori)

Maura: dark haired (Latin)

Maureen: dark skinned (French)

Maurise: dark haired, from the moor (French)

Mausi: picked flower (Native American)

Mauve: soft violet color (Greek)

Mavia: happy (Celtic)

Maxine: extreme, greatest (Latin)

May: born during the month of May, pink or white blossom (Latin)

Maya: dream, illusion (Hindi)

Maybell: great, worthy of love (Latin)

Mayda: woman (English)

Mayoree: beautiful Thai

Mayra: wind of spring (Aboriginal)

Maysun: beautiful (Arabic)

Mazal: lucky star (Hebrew)

Meade: honey wine (Greek)

Meagan: daisy (French); pearl (Greek); strength (Irish)

Megan: daisy (French); pearl (Greek); strength (Irish)

Meara: from the pool, laughter (Gaelic)

Meda: middle child (Latin); ruling (Greek)

Medina: city (Arabic)

Medora: ruler (Greek)

Mee: beautiful (Chinese)

Meena: mothers gift (Greek)

Meera: light (Israeli)

Meg: little pearl (Greek)

Megara: firstborn child (Greek)

Mehadi: flower (Hindi)

Mehira: energetic (Hebrew)

Meiko: flower bud (Japanese)

Mwinwen: slender (Welsh)

Meira: light (Hebrew)

Mejorana: sweet marjoram (Spanish)

Meka: child of purity (Greek); likeness to God (Hebrew)

Mel: sweet, like honey (Portuguese)

Mela: religious service (Hindi); dark haired (Polish)

Melanie: dark haired (Greek)

Melba: from the mill stream (Celtic); mallow flower (Latin); soft (Greek)

Mele: poem (Hawaiian)

Melecent: honeybee (Greek); strength (German)

Meleni: melon (Tongan)

Melesse: eternal (Ethiopian)

Melia: flower (Hawaiian)

Melina: canary yellow (Latin); honey (Greek)

Melinda: gentle (Greek); sweet, beautiful (Latin)

Meliora: better (Latin)

Melisande: determined strength (German)

Melissa: honeybee, sweet like honey (Greek)

Melita: aromatic oil, honeybee, honey-sweet (Greek)

Melody: music, song (Greek)

Melora: golden apple (Greek)

Melosa: beautiful song, sweet like honey (Spanish)

Melva: Mel's friend from the mill, chieftain (Gaelic); sword friend (English)

Melvina: Mel's friend from the mill, chieftain (Gaelic); sword friend (English)

Mena: strength (Dutch)

Menora: candle holder (Hebrew)

Meralda: emerald (Latin)

Mercedees: lady of mercies, reward (Spanish)

Mercia: compassionate, mercy (English); reward (Spanish)

Mercy: compassionate, mercy (English); reward (Spanish)

Meredith: from the sea, sea lord, great ruler (Welsh)

Mereki: peacemaker (Aboriginal)

Meri: rebellious (Hebrew)

Meriel: blackbird (Hebrew)

Merilyn: happy pool (English)

Merinda: beautiful (Aboriginal); happy (English)

Merie: blackbird (French)

Merrina: flour, plenty of grass seed (Aboriginal)

Merva: Mel's friend from the mill (Irish); sword friend (English)

Meryl: blackbird (Irish); famous (German); shining sea (Irish)

Mesha: born under the sign of Aries (Latin)

Messina: middle child, harvest (Latin)

Meta: ambition (Latin); land (Aboriginal)

Mhairie: wished for, star of the sea, bitter (Scottish)

Mia: mine (Italian)

Miandetta: bend in the river (Aboriginal)

Micah: child of purity (Greek); likeness to God (Hebrew)

Michelle: likeness to God (French)

Micina: new moon (Native American)

Midori: green (Japanese)

Mieko: prosperous (Japanese)

Miette: sweet little one (French)

Migina: new moon (Native American)

Mika: new moon (Japanese)

Miki: three trees growing together (Japanese); quick (Hawaiian)

Mila: from Milan (Italian); loved by the people (Slavic)

Milada: my lady (English); my love (Slavic)

Milena: mild (German)

Mileta: merciful (German); miller (Latin)

Mili: she is for me (Israeli)

Milia: hard-working (German)

Mililiani: heavenly caress (Hawaiian)

Milka: hard-working (German)

Millicent: strong worker (German)

Milly: hard-working, industrious (German)

Mima: woman (Burmese)

Mimi: my (French)

Mina: firstborn daughter (Native American); little, mine (English); love, loved memory (German)

Mindy: gentle (Greek); sweet (Latin)

Minerva: wisdom (Greek)

Minette: faithful defense (French)

Miniti: mint (Tongan)

Minka: little determined guardian (Polish)

Minkie: daylight (Aboriginal)

Minna: affectionate, tender (German)

Minowa: singer (Native American)

Minya: eldest sister (Native American)

Mio: strength three times over (Japanese)

Mira: beautiful, wonderful, prosperous (Latin)

Mirabel: beautiful, wonderful, prosperous (Latin)

Mirbabrook: Southern Cross constellation (Aboriginal)

Miranda: worthy of love, mermaid (Latin)

Mireil: God has spoken (Hebrew); wonderful (Latin)

Mirena: loved (Hawaiian)

Miri: wished for, star of the sea, bitter (Hebrew)

Miriam: strong willed, wished for, star of the sea, bitter (Hebrew)

Mirica: miracle child (Latin)

Mirna: polite (Irish)

Mirrin: cloud (Aboriginal)

Missy: little miss, honeybee, sweet like honey (English)

Misty: covered with a mist, concealed (English)

Mitzi: strong willed (German)

Miya: three arrows, temple (Japanese)

Miyoko: generations beautiful child (Japanese)

Miyuki: deep snow (Japanese)

Moana: the sea (Tongan); ocean (Hawaiian)

Modesty: gentle, modest (Latin)

Moesha: child (Egyptian); saved, taken from the water (Hebrew)

Mohala: flowering (Hawaiian)

Mohini: enchantress (Sanskrit)

Moina: advice (Latin); noble, aristocratic (Irish)

Mona: advice (Latin); noble, aristocratic (Irish)

Moira: fate (Greek); great, bitter (Gaelic)

Moli: orange (Tongan)

Molly: wishing (Hebrew); star of the sea (Latin)

Monica: adviser (Latin); solitary (Greek)

Monifa: lucky (African)

Monique: wise counsellor (French); advisor (Latin)

Mora: blueberry (Spanish)

Morasha: inheritance (Hebrew)

Moree: water (Aboriginal)

Moreen: great (Irish)

Morela: apricot (Polish)

Morena: brown haired (Spanish)

Morgan: of the sea (Celtic)

Morgwen: great fair hair (Welsh)

Moriah: dark haired (French); god is my teacher (Hebrew)

Morie: bay (Japanese)

Morina: mermaid (Irish)

Morissa: dark haired, from the moor (Latin)

Morna: affectionate, gentle (Gaelic); dawn (English)

Moselle: saved, taken from the water (French)

Mosina: saved, taken from the water (French)

Mouna: wish (Arabic)

Mrena: white eyes (Slavic)

Muna: saint (Basque)

Mura: village (Japanese)

Muriel: fragrant (Greek); sea bright (Irish)

Musetta: inspiration, muse, little bagpipe (French)

Musette: inspiration, muse, little bagpipe (French)

Mya: emerald (Burmese)

Mykaela: likeness to God (Hebrew)

Myla: merciful (English)

Myra: plenty (Greek); scented oil, myrrh (Latin); soft song (French)

Myrna: gentle, polite (Irish)

Myrrine: wind (Aboriginal)

N

Naarah: girl of my heart (Hebrew)

Nada: hope (Russian)

Nadia: hope (Russian)

Nadine: hope (Russian)

Nadalia: fire (Aboriginal)

Nadira: precious (Arabic)

Naeva: life (French)

Naia: dolphin (Hawaiian)

Nailah: successful (Arabic)

Nairi: from the land with canyons (Armenian)

Nakeisha: life (Swahili); woman (Arabic)

Nakeita: victory of the people (Russian)

Nakia: victory of the people (Russian)

Nalani: calm heavens, serenity of the skies (Hawaiian)

Nami: wave (Japanese)

Nanala: sunflower (Hawaiian)

Nancy: graceful (English)

Nanda: lake (Aboriginal)

Nanetta: little graceful one (French)

Nanette: little graceful one (French)

Naomi: pleasant (Hebrew)

Nara: happy (Irish); oak (Japanese)

Narcisse: daffodil, self-love (French)

Narelle: light, women from the sea (Aboriginal); from the north (Scandinavian)

Nari: thunder bolt (Japanese)

Narlala: look out (Aboriginal)

Narmanda: giver of pleasure (Hindi)

Nasya: miracle of God (Hebrew)

Nata: creator, speaker (Native American); dancer (Sanskrit); rope (Hindi)

Natalie: born on Christmas day (Latin)

Natane: daughter (Native American)

Natania: fairy queen found on Christmas day (Russian); gift of God (Hebrew)

Natara: sacrifice (Arabic)

Natasha: born on Christmas day (Russian); birthday (Latin)

Nathania: gift of God (Hebrew)

Nava: beautiful, lovely (Hebrew)

Navit: lovely, pleasant (Hebrew)

Naysa: miracle of God (Hebrew)

Neala: champion (Irish)

Neci: fiery (Hungarian)

Neda: child born on a Sunday (Slavic)

Neema: child born in prosperous times (Swahili)

Neheda: independent (Arabic)

Neige: snow (French)

Nekeisha: life (Swahili); woman (Hindi)

Nelda: from the elder tree home (English)

Nelia: horn colored, horn (Latin)

Nell: horn, sun ray (Latin)

Nellie: horn, sun ray (Latin)

Nenet: born by the sea (Egyptian)

Neola: youthful (Greek)

Neoma: new moon (Greek)

Nerida: red water lily (Aboriginal); sea nymph (Greek)

Nerina: black (Latin); sea nymph (Greek)

Nerine: sea fairy (Greek)

Nerys: lady (Welsh)

Nessa: headland, purity, butterfly (Norse)

Neta: plant (Hebrew)

Netta: little priceless one (Latin)

Neva: white (Spanish)

Neve: life (Hebrew)

Nevina: saint worshipper (Irish)

Neylan: wish which is fulfilled (Turkish)

Neysa: purity (Greek)

Nia: fairy (Irish)

Nichelle: likeness to God, victory of the people (French)

Nicki: victory of the people (Greek)

Nicky: victory of the people (Greek)

Nicola: victory of the people (Greek)

Nicole: victory of the people (Greek)

Nicoletta: little victory of the people (French)

Nicollete: little victory of the people (French)

Nidra: nest (Latin)

Niesha: friendly fairy (Scandinavian); life (African-American); alive and well (Arabic)

Nigella: champion (Gaelic); black, dark haired (Latin)

Nikah: belonging to God (Russian)

Nikita: victory of the people (Russian)

Nila: from the Nile (Latin)

Nili: indigo (Hebrew)

Nima: blessed (Arabic); thread (Hebrew)

Nina: little girl, great granddaughter (Spanish)

Ninetta: little girl, great granddaughter (Spanish)

Ninette: little girl, god has favored me (French)

Niree: family (Aboriginal)

Nirveli: child of water (Hindi)

Nishi: West (Japanese)

Nissa: friendly fairy, elf (Scandinavian); sign, to test (Hebrew); woman (Arabic)

Nita: bear (North American)

Nitara: roots run deep (Hindi)

Nitasha: child born on Christmas day (Russian)

Nitasse: resurrection (French)

Nitsa: shining light (Greek)

Noelani: beautiful one sent from heaven (Hawaiian)

Noeline: born at Christmas time (Latin); Christmas (French)

Nola: small bell, noble (Latin); white shoulders (Gaelic)

Nolana: small bell, noble (Latin); white shoulders (Gaelic)

Noma: ruler (Hawaiian)

Norma: ruler (Hawaiian)

Nona: ninth born child (Latin)

Noni: honestly (English); ninth (Latin)

Nora: light (Greek); woman of honor (Latin)

Noora: campsite (Aboriginal)

Norell: from the North (German)

Nori: belief, law, religious teachings (Japanese)

Norleen: honest (Irish)

Norna: Viking goddess of fate (Norse)

Nova: new (Latin)

Novella: newcomer, new (Latin)

Novia: new, youthful (Latin); sweetheart (Spanish)

Nuala: fair shoulders (Irish)

Nui: great (Maori)

Numa: beautiful (Arabic)

Nuna: land (Native American)

Nura: light (Aramaic)

Nuria: God's light (Aramaic)

Nurita: flower with yellow and red blossoms (Hebrew)

Nyah: river bend (Aboriginal)

Nydia: next, safe refuge (Latin)

Nyora: cherry tree (Aboriginal)

Nyree: sea (Maori)

Nyssa: beginning (Greek); one who has goals (Latin)

O

Obelia: strength (Greek)

Odele: melody, song (French)

Odelette: little song lyric (French)

Odelia: one who lives in the valley (English); praise to God (Hebrew); little, wealthy (Scandinavian)

Odette: home lover (French); of the fatherland (German)

Ofira: golden (Hebrew)

Ohanna: God is gracious (Hebrew)

Ohara: small field (Japanese)

Ohnicio: honorable (Irish)

Okalani: sent from heaven (Hawaiian)

Oketa: orchard (Tongan)

Okilani: heaven (Hawaiian)

Ola: ancestral relic (Scandinavian); life, well-being (Nigerian)

Olabasi: increasing (Nigerian)

Olalla: speaking sweetly (Greek)

Olanthe: beautiful (Native American)

Oleatha: light (Scandinavian)

Olena: light (Russian)

Olesia: protector of human kind (Polish)

Olga: holy (Scandinavian)

Oliana: oleander (Polynesian)

Olienka: holy (Russian)

Olina: happy (Hawaiian)

Olinda: sweetly scented (Latin)

Olisa: God's promise (Hebrew)

Olive: olive tree (Latin)

Olivia: olive tree (Latin)

Olono: hill (Aboriginal)

Olwyn: old friend (English); white footprints (Welsh)

Olympia: heavenly, of Olympus (Greek)

Oma: high commander, follower of the prophet (Arabic)

Omaira: red (Arabic)

Omemee: picture (Native American)

Ona: graceful (Lithuanian); donkey (Greek); unity (Latin)

Onawa: wide awake girl (Native American)

Ondine: wave of water (Latin)

Ondrea: brave woman (Slavic)

Oneida: one who is expected (Native American)

Onella: shining light (Hungarian)

Onesta: honest, reliable (English)

Oni: God has favored me (Hebrew)

Onida: desired (Native American)

Onora: honesty (English)

Oola: fireplace (Aboriginal)

Oona: lamb (Irish); one (Latin)

Opal: gem, precious jewel (Sanskrit)

Opeli: opal gem (Tongan)

Ophelia: help (Greek)

Ophra: young deer, place of dust (Hebrew)

Oprah: young deer, place of dust (Hebrew)

Ora: coastal shoreline (English); golden light (Hebrew); golden prayer (Latin)

Orabel: golden beauty (French)

Orah: light (Hebrew)

Oralee: light (Hebrew); speaker from the meadow (English)

Oralia: golden (Latin)

Orana: welcome (Aboriginal)

Orazia: timekeeper (Italian)

Orchio: orchid flower child (Italian)

Orea: from the mountain (Greek)

Orela: divine announcement (Latin)

Orell: eagle (Russian); listener (Latin); from the hill of ore (English)

Oretha: virtuous (Greek)

Oriana: golden dawn (Latin)

Oriel: fire (German); golden (Latin)

Oriella: white skin (Celtic)

Orina: peaceful (Russian)

Orinda: light skin (Irish); pine tree (Hebrew)

Orino: worker in the field (Japanese)

Oriole: blonde, fair-haired, golden (Latin)

Orla: golden (Irish)

Orlena: golden (Latin)

Orlenda: eagle (Russian)

Orli: light (Hebrew)

Ormanda: noble (Latin); sailor (German)

Orna: decorated (Latin); light olive color (Irish)

Ornice: cedar tree (Hebrew); olive color (Irish)

Orpah: fawn (Hebrew)

Orsa: little she-bear (Greek)

Orseline: little she-bear (Dutch)

Orva: friend with a spear, worth gold (French)

Orwin: boar friend (Hebrew)

Orya: peaceful (Russian)

Osanna: merciful, prayer (Latin)

Osen: one thousand (Japanese)

Oseye: happy (African)

Osita: divine strength (Spanish)

Osma: divine protector (English)

Osyka: eagle (Native American)

Otilie: lucky (Slavic)

Ottavia: eight born child (Italian); eighth (Latin)

Ovia: egg (Latin)

Ozara: treasured, wealth (Hebrew)

Ozera: helper (Hebrew)

P

Paige: attendant, young child (English)

Pala: kitten (Swahili)

Paloma: dove (Spanish)

Pam: loving, sweet, honey (Greek)

Pancha: freedom (Spanish)

Panchali: princess of Panchala (Sanskrit)

Pandora: all gifts (Greek)

Pania: sea woman (Maori)

Panisi: pansy flower (Tongan)

Pansy: idea (French); little flower (Greek)

Panthea: all gods (Greek)

Papina: oak tree with a vine (Native American)

Paris: capital of France (French)

Parthena: purity (Greek)

Parvati: mountain climber (Sanskrit)

Pascale: born at Easter time, passover (French)

Pascha: passover (French)

Pat: twisted willows (Native American)

Patsy: little noble one (Latin)

Patty: noble (Latin)

Patience: enduring, patient (Latin)

Patrice: little noble one (Latin)

Patricia: little noble one (Latin)

Patya: flower (Aboriginal)

Paula: small (Latin)

Paulette: small (Latin)

Paulina: small (Latin)

Pauline: small (Latin)

Pazia: gold, golden haired (Hebrew)

Peaches: peach tree (English)

Pearl: pearl (English)

Peata: one who brings joy (Maori)

Peggy: daisy (French); pearl (Greek)

Preilla: God has added (Spanish)

Peita: stone, rock (Greek)

Peta: stone, rock (Greek)

Peneli: penny coin, weaver (Greek)

Penelope: penny coin, weaver (Greek)

Penny: penny coin, weaver (Greek)

Penthea: fifth born child, fifth (Greek)

Peony: flower, giver of praise, god of healing (Greek)

Pepe: butterfly (Tongan)

Pepita: bountiful (Spanish)

Perette: little stone (French)

Peri: prosperous (Greek)

Perilla: stone (Latin)

Perizada: born of the ferries (Persian)

Perlita: pearl (Italian)

Pernella: stone (Greek)

Perry: pear tree (French)

Persis: from Persia (Greek)

Petica: noble (Latin)

Petra: stone (Greek)

Petrina: steady (Greek)

Petula: seeker (Latin)

Petunia: sweetly scented flower (Native American)

Phanessa: butterfly (Greek)

Phedra: brightly shining (Greek)

Phelia: immortal wisdom (Greek)

Philana: lover of humankind (Greek)

Philantha: lover of flowers (Greek)

Philippa: horse lover (Greek)

Philomela: lover of songs (Greek)

Philomena: she is loved (Greek)

Phoebe: bright, shining, pure (Greek)

Phylicia: happy one from the green town (Latin)

Phyllis: green, leafy branch (Greek)

Pia: devout, pious (Italian)

Pierette: little steady one (French); stone (Greek)

Pililani: near to heaven (Hawaiian)

Piper: pipe layer (English)

Pipipa: sand piper (Aboriginal)

Pippa: lover of horses (Greek)

Pippi: rosy cheeked (French)

Piscina: pool of water (Italian)

Pita: fourth born child (Italian)

Pixie: little fairy (English)

Poeta: poetry (Italian)

Pola: sunlight (Greek)

Polla: poppy flower (Arabic)

Polly: star of the sea, many (Hebrew)

Pollyana: star of the sea (Hebrew); sees the bright side of a situation (English)

Poloma: bow (Native American)

Poppy: poppy flower, grandfather (English)

Portia: offering, sweet wine (Latin); from the town by the water (English)

Posala: flower (Native American)

Preya: prayer (Latin)

Primrose: primrose flower, first rose (English)

Priscilla: ancient (Latin)

Prisma: cut, saw (Greek)

Priya: loved, sweet natured (Latin)

Pru: cautious, discretion (Latin)

Prudence: cautious, discretion (Latin)

Prue: cautious, discretion (Latin)

Pua: flower (Hawaiian)

Puakai: sea flower (Hawaiian)

Puakea: white flower (Hawaiian)

Pualani: heavenly flower (Hawaiian)

Purity: purity (English)

Pyralis: fire (Greek)

Pyrena: fiery (Greek)

Q

Qadesh: Egyptian goddess (Egyptian)

Qadiri: powerful (Arabic)

Quaneisha: life (Swahili); woman (Arabic)

Quiana: graceful (Hebrew)

Quinta: fifth born child (Latin)

Quintana: fifth born child (Latin); from the Queen's lawn (English)

Quintessa: essence (Latin)

Quintina: fifth born child (Latin)

Quirita: citizen (Latin)

R

Raama: one who trembles (Hebrew)

Raanana: fresh (Hebrew)

Rachelle: ewe, lamb (French)

Rachel: ewe, lamb (French)

Raquel: ewe, lamb (French)

Radella: counsellor (English)

Radwa: mountain (Arabic)

Rae: doe, ewe (English)

Raelene: rule temptress (Latin)

Rafaela: God has healed (Hebrew)

Raphaela: God has healed (Hebrew)

Raina: powerful (German); rainy (English)

Raine: queen (Latin); carefree (Greek)

Raisa: rose (Hebrew); carefree (Greek)

Raizel: rose (Hebrew)

Raissa: believer, thinker (French)

Rajani: evening (Hindi)

Ramona: wise protector, protecting hands (Spanish); frog (Spanish); beautiful, eye catching (Arabic)

Rana: catcher (Scandinavian); worthy of admission (Latin)

Randa: tree (Arabic)

Randi: invincible, shield (English)

Rane: queen (Scandinavian)

Rani: happy, she is singing (Hebrew); queen (Scandinavian)

Rania: happy, she is singing (Hebrew)

Ranielle: God is my judge (Hebrew)

Raniyah: gazing (Arabic)

Rasha: young gazelle (Arabic)

Rasia: rose (Greek)

Ratana: crystal Thai

Ratri: night (Hindi)

Raven: black, black haired, large black bird (English)

Ravva: sun (Hindi)

Rawiya: storyteller (Arabic)

Raya: friend (Hebrew)

Rayann: royal grace (French)

Rayleen: from the royal meadow (French); purity (Hebrew)

Rayna: mighty (Scandinavian)

Rea: poppy flower (Greek)

Reade: adviser (English)

Reanna: mighty grace (German)

Reba: bound, faithful (Hebrew)

Rebecca: bound, faithful (Hebrew)

Rechaba: rider of horses (Hebrew)

Reena: peace (Greek)

Regina: queen (Latin)

Rei: polite, well-behaved (Japanese)

Reiko: grateful (Japanese)

Reina: queen (Spanish)

Rena: joyful song (Hebrew)

Renata: song of joy (Hebrew)

Rene: peace (Greek)

Renee: reborn (French)

Renita: rebel (Latin)

Renni: song (Hebrew)

Renny: prosperous one (Irish)

Retha: best (Greek)

Reubena: behold: a daughter (Hebrew); renewed strength (Latin)

Reva: rain (Hebrew)

Revaya: satisfaction (Hebrew)

Rewa: slender, tall (Polynesian)

Reyhan: sweet smelling flower (Polynesian); late Summer (Greek)

Reza: harvester (Slavic); well spoken (Greek)

Rheta: ardent, enthusiastic (Welsh)

Rhiamon: goddess, wisdom (Welsh)

Rhian: God's gracious woman (Welsh); goddess, great queen (Welsh)

Rhiannon: sorceress (Gaelic)

Rhodah: from Rhodes, from where the roses grow (Greek)

Rhodelia: rose, rosy cheeked (Greek)

Rhonda: powerful, good lance (Welsh)

Rhonwen: rose, white friend (Celtic)

Ria: small river (Spanish)

Rianna: virtuous strength, great queen (Irish)

Ricca: ruler (Spanish)

Richael: saint (Irish)

Richelle: rich and powerful (German)

Ricki: rich powerful ruler, peaceful ruler (German)

Rida: God has favored her (Arabic)

Riddhi: prosperous (Sanskrit)

Rihana: sweet basil herb (Arabic)

Rika: ruler (Swedish)

Riley: courageous, valiant (Irish)

Rilla: stream (German)

Rima: poetry, rhyme (Spanish)

Rimona: pomegranate, plant with red fruit (Arabic)

Rina: happy, song (Hebrew)

Riona: queen, saintly (Irish)

Rihsa: laughing (Latin)

Rissa: see fairy (Greek); daisy (French); pear (Greek)

Rita: brave strength (Hindi); to bind (Hebrew)

Riva: from the riverbank, shore (French); to bind (Hebrew)

River: from the riverbank, shore (French)

Riverlea: from the river meadow (Latin)

Riza: harvester (Greek)

Roannah: graceful rose (Hebrew); bright fame (German)

Robin: robin bird (English)

Rochelle: she is a little like a rock (French)

Rocio: dew (Latin)

Roesia: rose (French); little rock, rest (German)

Rohana: sandalwood (Hindi)

Rohini: woman (Hindi)

Roisin: rose (Irish)

Rokeya: dawn (Persian)

Rolanda: renowned in the land (Latin)

Roma: from Rome (Roman)

Romaine: from Rome (Roman)

Romana: from Rome (Roman)

Romilda: from Rome (Roman)

Romina: from Rome (Roman)

Romelda: Roman warrior (German)

Romia: highly praised (Hebrew)

Romola: lady from Rome (Latin); seal (Irish); song of joy (Hebrew)

Rona: rough island (Norse)

Ronaele: shining light (Greek)

Ronalda: powerful (Norse)

Roneisha: grand life (Welsh)

Ronelle: she is grand (Welsh)

Ronena: my song is happiness (Hebrew)

Roni: happy (Hebrew)

Roniya: God's happiness (Hebrew)

Ronli: happy (Hebrew); famous rule (Irish)

Rori: aurora, dawn (Latin); famous rule (Irish)

Rory: aurora, dawn (Latin)

Rosa: rose (Latin)

Rosabelle: beautiful rose (Latin)

Rosalba: white rose (Latin)

Rosalee: from the rose meadow (Latin); lovely rose (German)

Rosalind: little rose (Irish); rose of the world (French)

Rosamond: famous prophet (German)

Rosanna: graceful rose (English)

Rosaria: rosary (Italian)

Rosario: rosary (Italian)

Rose: rose flower (English)

Rosie: rose flower (English)

Roseanne: pretty roses (English)

Roselani: heavenly rose Filipino

Rosemary: rosemary herb, dew of the sea (Latin)

Rosetta: little rose (Latin)

Roshan: shining light (Sanskrit)

Rosina: rose (English)

Rosita: rose (Spanish); from the rose pool (English)

Rossalyn: from the cape (Scottish)

Roula: rebel (Greek)

Royanna: gracious queen (English)

Roz: fair rose (Spanish)

Roza: rose (Slavic)

Rozelle: she is a rose (Greek)

Ruana: musical instrument (Hindi); red (Latin)

Ruby: ruby, gem (French)

Rudelle: she is famous (French)

Rudi: famous wolf, flame (German)

Rudy: famous wolf, flame (German)

Rudra: seeds (Hindi); street (French); strong herbs (English)

Rue: famous (German)

Rufina: red haired (Italian)

Rui: affectionate (Japanese)

Rukan: confident (Arabic)

Rukiya: rising (Swahili)

Rula: ruler (Latin)

Runa: following secret (Norse)

Ruri: emerald (Japanese)

Ruta: friendly (Hawaiian); kindhearted, friend, companion (Hebrew)

Ruth: compassionate (English)

Ruza: rose (Slavic)

Ryann: king (Irish)

Rylee: courageous, valiant (Irish)

Ryo: dragon (Japanese)

S

Saada: one who gives support (Hebrew)

Saarah: princess (Arabic); old (Hebrew); woman from Sheba (Greek)

Saba: morning (Arabic)

Sabara: thorny cactus (Hebrew)

Sabbatha: child born on a Sunday (Hebrew)

Sabina: Sabines [an Italian tribe during the Roman era] (Latin)

Sabiya: morning East wind (Arabic)

Sable: soft fur (English); thorny (Hebrew)

Sabra: restful (Arabic)

Sabrina: boundary (Latin)

Sacha: defender of humankind (Greek)

Sachi: bringer of bliss (Japanese)

Sada: seed (English); honor confers a crown (African)

Sade: princess (Hebrew)

Sadie: princess (Hebrew)

Sadhana: devoted (Hindi); star (Arabic)

Sadira: lily (Persian)

Sadiya: lucky (Arabic)

Safa: purity (Arabic)

Safaia: blue, sapphire (Tongan)

Saffi: wisdom (Danish)

Saffron: yellow, orange (Arabic)

Safiya: best friend, purity (Arabic)

Sage: healthy wisdom, wise (Latin)

Sahar: dawn (Arabic); talented (Japanese)

Sai: good (Tongan)

Saidah: happy, lucky (Arabic)

Sakae: wealthy (Japanese)

Sakara: sweet (Native American)

Sakti: energy (Hindi)

Sakuna: bird (Native American)

Sakura: cherry blossom, wealthy (Japanese)

Sala: sacred tree (Hindi)

Salali: squirrel (Native American)

Salama: peaceful (Arabic)

Salato: tree (Tongan)

Sale: princess (Hawaiian); moon (Hindi)

Salena: princess (English)

Salette: little princess, little Sally (English)

Salida: happy (Hebrew)

Salihah: purity (Arabic)

Salima: safe (Arabic)

Salina: solemn (French)

Salliann: graceful princess (English)

Sally: princess (Hebrew)

Salma: one who is safe (Swahili)

Salwa: bringer of comfort (Arabic)

Sam: asked for, her name is God, listening (Hebrew)

Samala: asked for, her name is God (Hebrew)

Samantha: god heard, god is listening (Hebrew)

Samar: guarded, one who talks at night (Arabic)

Samara: guarded, one who talks at night (Arabic)

Samariah: guarded, one who talks at night (Arabic); listening (Hebrew)

Sameh: for giving (Arabic)

Samena: secret (Tongan); praised (Arabic)

Sami: asked for (Hebrew)

Samia: one who understands (Arabic); little Sam, little asked for one (Hebrew)

Samina: happiness (Hindi)

Samira: entertainer (Arabic)

Samuela: asked for, her name is God (Hebrew)

Samya: rising (Hebrew); mountain top (Arabic)

Sana: lily (Hebrew)

Sananda: happiness (Hindi)

Sanchia: sacred purity (Latin)

Sandra: defender of humankind (English)

Sandre: defender of humankind (English)

Sandy: defender of humankind (English)

Sandyha: twilight (Hindi)

Sangata: saint (Tongan)

Sanjana: knowing right from wrong (Sanskrit)

Sanne: lily flower (Hebrew)

Sansana: palm tree leaf (Hebrew)

Santana: saint, holy (Spanish)

Santavana: hope (Hindi)

Santillana: soft haired (Spanish)

Santina: little saint (Spanish)

Sanura: kitten (Swahili)

Sanuye: red clouds in the sunset (Native American)

Sanya: born on a Saturday (Sanskrit)

Sanyu: happy (Native American)

Sapata: dancing bear (Native American)

Sapphire: blue, sapphire (Greek)

Sapphira: blue, sapphire (Greek)

Sappi: wisdom Lithuanian

Sara: princess (Hebrew)

Sarala: straight (Hindi)

Saranu: fast runner (Sanskrit)

Saree: princess (Hebrew)

Sari: princess (Hebrew)

Sarice: princess (Hebrew)

Sarika: princess (Hebrew)

Saril: flowing water (Turkish)

Sarila: waterfall (Turkish); serene, calm (Latin)

Sarina: princess (Hebrew); serene, calm (Latin)

Sarinha: princess (Hebrew)

Sarita: princess (Hebrew)

Saronna: princess, from the plains (Hebrew)

Sarotte: little princess (French)

Sasa: princess (Hungarian)

Sasha: defender of humankind (Russian)

Sasona: happy (Hebrew)

Sass: wrote, cheeky, Saxon (Irish)

Satara: princess from the rocky hill (Hebrew)

Satin: shiny, smooth (French)

Satini: satin (Tongan)

Satinka: sacred dancer (Native American)

Sato: sugar, sweet (Japanese)

Sauda: dark skinned (Swahili)

Saula: asked for, borrowed (Hebrew)

Saundra: defender of humankind (Greek)

Saura: worshipper of the sun (Hindi)

Savanna: open grassland (Latin)

Savina: from Sabines (Latin)

Savitri: one who provokes (Sanskrit)

Sawa: swamp (Japanese)

Sawni: echo (Native American)

Sayo: born during the night (Japanese)

Scarlett: red color (English)

Scienta: knowledge, scientist (Latin)

Seana: God is gracious (Irish)

Sebastiana: honored above all others (Greek)

Secelia: unseeing, blind (Latin)

Seelia: unseeing, blind (Latin)

Seda: one who hears the voices of the forest (Armenian)

Sedna: goddess of the sea, well fed (Eskimo)

Seema: sign, symbol (Greek)

Seiko: accomplished (Japanese)

Seini: God is gracious (Polynesian)

Seiran: bright, sparkling (Welsh)

Seki: wonderful (Japanese)

Sela: stone (Hebrew)

Selam: peace (Ethiopian)

Selda: rare (English)

Selena: heavenly, moon (Greek)

Selene: heavenly, moon (Greek)

Selina: heavenly, moon (Greek)

Selima: peace (Hebrew); guarded, divinely protected (Scandinavian); secure (Arabic)

Selma: fair haired (Celtic)

Sema: heaven (Tongan)

Semira: tall as the heavens (Hebrew)

Sena: hospitable, guest (Greek)

Seona: God is gracious (Scottish)

Serah: pour (Hebrew)

Seraphina: seraph, highest order of the angels (Hebrew)

Serena: peace, serene, calm (Latin)

Serene: peace, serene, calm (Latin)

Serenity: peace, serene, calm (Latin)

Serita: little princess (Hebrew)

Sesheta: goddess of stars (Egyptian)

Sevilla: prophet, wise woman (Spanish)

Shaanana: peace (Hebrew)

Shada: pelican (Native American)

Shadya: singer (Arabic)

Shae: admirable (Gaelic)

Shay: admirable (Gaelic)

Shea: admirable (Gaelic)

Shaelea: from the fairy palace in the meadow (Irish)

Shaelyn: from the fairy palace pool (Irish)

Shahar: born on a moonlit night (Arabic)

Shahina: falcon (Arabic)

Shahira: famous (Arabic)

Shahla: beautiful eyes (Afghani)

Shaila: mountain that is small (Hindi)

Shaina: beautiful (Hebrew)

Shaine: beautiful (Hebrew)

Shakara: she is purity Danish

Shakeena: she is brave, quick (Irish); energy circle (Sanskrit)

Shakeia: beginning of the season, unknown (African); energy circle (Sanskrit)

Shakia: beginning of the season, unknown (African)

Shakeita: from the woods (Scottish)

Shakela: dweller from the farm near the woods, warrior (Irish)

Shakila: she is the pretty one (Arabic)

Shakira: thankful, grateful (Arabic)

Shakti: divine (Hindi); light, handsome, happy (Hawaiian)

Shalana: attractive (Irish); woman (Arabic)

Shaleisha: life (Swahili); dwelling (Hebrew)

Shalena: distinguished, famous (Norwegian)

Shalisa: honeybee (Hebrew)

Shalita: happy (Latin)

Shalona: lioness (Latin)

Shalonda: water fairy (Latin)

Shalva: peace (Hebrew)

Shalyn: from the shade pool (Welsh)

Shamara: battle ready warrior (Arabic)

Shameena: beautiful (Hindi)

Shameka: likeness to God (Hebrew); wonderful (Latin)

Shamira: to gaze (Spanish)

Shammara: battle prepared warrior (Arabic)

Shana: God is gracious, lily, rose (Hebrew)

Shanae: God is gracious, lily, rose (Hebrew)

Shanda: goddess (Sanskrit)

Shandra: defender of humankind (Greek)

Shandy: noisy (English)

Shanelle: she is from the channel (French)

Shaneta: plant (Hebrew)

Shania: I'm on my way (Native American)

Shanice: God is gracious (Hebrew); prosperous (English)

Shanida: hard-working (German)

Shanie: beautiful (Hebrew)

Shanika: belonging to God (Russian)

Shanisa: God is gracious, sign (Hebrew); planter (Hebrew)

Shanita: bear (Native American); slow water (Celtic)

Shanna: God is gracious (Hebrew)

Shannon: old, ancient (Gaelic)

Shanta: song (French)

Shantaina: saintly (Spanish)

Shantana: saint (Spanish)

Shantara: from the rocky hill (Irish)

Shanteca: harvester (Hungarian)

Shantelle: stone (French)

Shantille: stone (French)

Shantesa: harvester (Greek)

Shantia: God's gracious princess (Greek)

Shantina: little Christian (Latin)

Shantrice: song (French)

Shara: princess, fertile plain (Hebrew)

Sharae: princess (Hebrew)

Sharda: runs away (English); runaway (Arabic)

Shardae: charitable (Hindi)

Shareene: from the graceful plains (Hebrew)

Shrai: beloved (French)

Sharice: song of happiness, cherry (French)

Sharik: child of God (African); free man (German)

Sharleen: song of happiness (French)

Sharlote: little strong and courageous woman (French)

Scharmaine: song (Latin)

Sharna: from the plains (Hebrew)

Sharolyn: princess from the pool (Hebrew)

Sharon: from the plains (Hebrew)

Shatara: from the rocky hill (Irish)

Shauna: God is gracious (Irish)

Shaunta: God is gracious (Irish)

Shavonda: admired (Irish)

Shawanna: wanderer (German)

Shawna: God is gracious (Irish)

Shawndelle: God is gracious to her (Irish)

Shayla: from the fairy palace (Gaelic)

Shayna: beautiful one from the fairy palace (Yiddish)

Sheba: promise, queen, seventh daughter (Hebrew)

Sheena: God has favored (Irish)

Sheila: feminine, woman (Australian)

Sheina: gift from God (Hebrew)

Shelley: belonging to the meadow of shells (English)

Sheona: she is unity (Irish)

Sher: shrine (English)

Shera: light (Aramaic)

Sherelle: she is loved (French)

Sheri: free man, dear, loved (French)

Sheridan: seeker (Gaelic)

Sherika: one who listens, family (Arabic)

Sherilyn: from the beloved cool (Celtic)

Sherissa: beloved (French)

Sherita: beloved (French)

Sherry: cherished (French)

Sheryl: beloved (Welsh)

Sheyenne: graceful oak (French)

Shika: gentle deer (Japanese)

Shilo: gift of God (Hebrew)

Shina: victorious (Japanese)

Shinae: goddess gracious, reborn (Irish)

Shiona: God is gracious (Hebrew)

Shiquita: little girl (Spanish)

Shiri: my song (Hebrew)

Shirley: bright meadow and sunny clearing (English)

Shizu: quiet (Japanese)

Shona: God has favored (Irish)

Shura: defender of humankind (Russian)

Shyla: shy (English)

Siana: from China (Tongan)

Siale: flowering bush (Tongan)

Siany: health (Irish)

Sibena: alluring, siren (Greek)

Sibyl: prophet, wise woman (Greek)

Sidba: shining like a star (Latin); cloth of fine linen (Greek)

Sidonia: enchantress (Phoenician)

Sidra: star (Latin); mountain (Arabic); saw toothed (Spanish)

Sierra: black (Irish)

Siete: black, dark, jet stone (Tongan); sign or symbol (Latin)

Signa: conquering guardian (Norse)

Sigourney: conquer who is victorious (English)

Sigrid: beautiful victory (Norse)

Siham: arrow (Arabic)

Sikota: kingfisher bird (Tongan)

Silika: silk (Tongan); woods, forest (Latin)

Silvia: silver (Tongan)

Silvana: silver, girl from the woods (Italian)

Silvia: silver, girl from the woods (Latin)

Simone: listening (Hebrew)

Somoriah: watcher (Hebrew)

Sindy: little ashes (Greek)

Sinead: God has favored (Irish)

Siobhain: admired (Irish)

Sirena: alluring siren (Greek)

Siri: tranquil (Scandinavian)

Sirri: princess (Finnish)

Sisika: songbird (Native American)

Sissy: sister (English); trench (Sanskrit)

Sita: cedar tree (Tongan)

Siti: woman of respect (Swahili)

Sivanah: born during the ninth month of the Jewish year (Israeli)

Sivia: deer (Hebrew)

Sky: blue sky, heavenly (English)

Sloane: warrior (Scottish)

Socorro: one who helps (Spanish)

Sofia: wisdom (Greek)

Solace: comfort during a time of unhappiness (Latin)

Solada: listening (Thai); sunshine (Spanish)

Solana: easterly wind (Latin); solemn (French); sun angel (French)

Solange: alone (Latin)

Soleil: sunflower (French)

Solenne: dignified, solemn (French); sunlight, eastern wind (Spanish)

Solina: moon (Greek)

Solita: accustomed, used to (Latin); luna (Hindi)

Soma: body (Greek)

Sona: noisy (Latin)

Sondra: defender of humankind (Greek)

Sonel: lily (Hebrew)

Sonia: wisdom (Greek)

Sophia: wisdom (French)

Sophie: wisdom (Greek)

Sora: songbird (Native American)

Soraya: princess (Persian)

Sorrell: reddish brown color (French)

Souzan: fire (Persian)

Spira: round basket (Greek)

Stacey: resurrection, springtime (Greek)

Stacia: resurrection, springtime (Greek)

Starla: star (English)

Starlee: from the star meadow (English)

Starling: starling bird (English)

Stefanida: crowned (Russian)

Stefannia: crowned (Greek)

Steffi: crowned, garland (Greek)

Stella: star (Latin)

Stephanie: crowned (Greek)

Stevana: crowned (Greek)

Stevie: crowned (Greek)

Stina: Christian (German)

Sudy: southerly wind (English)

Sue: lily (Hebrew)

Sue-Ellen: lily of the shining light (Scottish)

Suela: consolation (Spanish)

Suhaila: gentle (Arabic)

Sujata: noble (Hindi)

Suka: sugar (Tongan)

Sukey: lily (Hawaiian)

Suki: beloved (Japanese)

Sula: large seabird (Icelandic)

Sulia: youthful (Latin)

Suma: asked for (Tanzanian); from the summer meadow (English)

Sumalee: beautiful flower (Thai)

Sumati: unity (Hindi)

Sumi: elegant (Japanese)

Sumiko: beautiful trial (Japanese)

Summer: born during summer (English); happy (English)

Sunee: good (Thai)

Sunita: behaved (Hindi)

Sunki: successful hunter, swift (Native American)

Sunniva: some gift (Scandinavian)

Sunny: bright, happy (English)

Sunshine: shining (English)

Surata: blessed happiness (Pakistani)

Suri: princess (Hebrew)

Surya: sun god (Pakistani)

Susammi: beloved lily (French)

Susan: graceful lily (Hebrew)

Susannah: graceful lily (Hebrew)

Susie: lily (Hebrew)

Sutki: broken pot (Native American)

Suzette: little lily (French)

Svea: southerly wind Swedish

Svetlana: star light (Russian)

Sya: summer (Chinese)

Sybil: prophet (Greek)

Sydelle: princess (Hebrew)

Syke: mulberry tree (Greek)

Sylwen: from the forest (Latin)

Syona: happiness (Hindi)

T

Tabia: talented (Swahili)

Tabitha: graceful gazelle (Aramaic)

Tacey: peaceful silence (English)

Tacita: silence (Latin); praising God (Hebrew)

Taddea: courageous (Greek)

Tadia: courageous (Greek)

Taesha: happy (Latin)

Taffy: much loved (Welsh)

Taffine: much loved (Welsh)

Tafne: goddess of light (Egyptian)

Tahi: seawater (Tongan)

Tahira: purity (Arabic); little (English)

Tahnee: dairy queen (Russian)

Taika: tiger (Tongan)

Taima: loud thunder (Native American)

Taimani: diamonds (Tongan)

Tain: new moon (Hawaiian)

Tais: bound together (Greek)

Taja: crown (Sanskrit)

Taka: one who was honored (Japanese)

Takara: precious treasure (Japanese)

Takeko: bamboo (Japanese)

Takenya: falcon (Native American)

Taki: waterfall (Japanese)

Takia: one who worships (Arabic)

Takina: carried away (Tongan); sun (Persian)

Takira: light (Latin)

Takota: friendly to all, stalking wolf (Native American)

Tala: seagull (Tongan)

Taleah: from the meadow with the tall trees (English)

Taleisha: life (Swahili); hard-working (Norse); temptress (Latin)

Talena: home (Hebrew); waiting (Tongan)

Tali: dew (Hebrew); gentle dew drops from heaven (Hebrew)

Talia: flowering (Greek)

Taliba: knowledge seeker (Arabic)

Talise: beautiful water (Native American); woman (Arabic)

Talitha: child (Hebrew)

Tallara: rain (Aboriginal)

Tallulah: leaping running water (Native American)

Tally: child (Hebrew); small hill (Hebrew)

Talma: crash of thunder (Native American)

Talor: morning dew drops (Hebrew)

Talya: little lamb (Hebrew); polished jewel (Japanese)

Tama: palm tree, pigeon (Hebrew)

Tamah: wonder (Hebrew)

Tamara: perfection, date fruit, palm tree (Hebrew)

Tamasina: twin (Aramaic)

Tamassa: twin (Aramaic)

Tamath: slow pace (Arabic)

Tameka: twin (Hebrew)

Tamesha: born under the sign of Aries (Hindi); perfection, palm tree (Hebrew)

Tami: people (Japanese)

Tamila: dearest (Russian)

Tammy: affection, date palm (Hebrew)

Tamra: date palm (Hebrew)

Tana: ceremony (Aboriginal)

Tanay: daughter (Hindi)

Tanaya: daughter (Hindi)

Taneya: fairy queen (Russian)

Tangia: angel (Greek); valley (Japanese)

Tani: make famous (Spanish)

Tania: fairy queen (Russian)

Tanya: fairy queen (Russian)

Taniel: God is my judge (Hebrew)

Tanisha: fairy queen (Russian)

Tanita: one who plants (Hebrew)

Tanith: goddess of love (Venetian)

Tannis: fairy queen (Slavic); measure (Arabic); hill, star (Gaelic)

Tara: carry (Aramaic)

Taral: ripple (Hindi)

Taraneh: melody (Persian)

Tari: from the rocky hill (Irish)

Tarne: mountain lake (Scandinavian)

Tarni: salt water (Aboriginal)

Taryn: from the peaceful rocky hill (Irish)

Tasaria: child born at sunrise (Gypsy); birthday (Russian)

Tasha: born on Christmas day (Latin)

Tashelle: nativity, likeness to God (Hebrew)

Tashi: bird flying (Native American)

Tasida: horse rider (Native American); twin (Hebrew)

Tasma: born on Christmas day (Slavic)

Tasmin: twin (Hebrew)

Tata: fairy queen (Russian)

Tate: happy (English)

Tatiana: fairy queen (Russian)

Tauba: dove (German)

Taula: priestess (Tongan)

Tautiti: graceful dancer (Polynesian)

Tavia: eight born child (Latin)

Tawanna: wandering (German)

Tawia: child born after twins (African)

Taya: home in the valley field (Japanese)

Tayanita: beaver (Native American)

Taylea: from the tall meadow (English)

Taylor: tailor, to cut (English); doe (Celtic)

Teagan: beautiful (English)

Tegan: beautiful (English)

Teangi: earthy (Aboriginal)

Teanna: graceful (English)

Teca: harvester (Hungarian)

Tecia: God's famous one (Greek)

Tecla: divine, famous (Greek)

Teddi: wealthy ruling guardian (English)

Telae: fish (Tongan)

Temina: honest (Arabic)

Tempany: storm (Latin)

Temperance: moderation (Latin)

Tempest: storm, turbulent (French)

Templa: temple (Latin)

Tennille: champion (Irish)

Tera: earth (Latin)

Teralyn: from the land by the pool (Latin)

Terelle: she is the harvester (Greek)

Terentia: smooth, tender (Greek)

Teresa: harvester, late summer (Greek)

Teri: harvester, late summer (Greek)

Terry: harvester, late summer (Greek)

Theresa: harvester, late summer (Greek)

Therese: harvester, late summer (Greek)

Terra: land, earthy (Latin)

Terrene: swiftly moving arrow (Japanese)

Teruma: gift (Hebrew)

Tess: harvester, fourth born child, late Summer (Greek)

Tessa: fourth child (Greek)

Thalassa: sea, ocean (Greek)

Thalia: flowering, flourishing (Greek)

Thamah: honest (Hebrew)

Thamar: palm tree, date fruit (Hebrew)

Thana: happy time (Arabic)

Thea: divine, goddess (Greek)

Theano: divine name (Greek)

Thelma: wilful (Greek)

Theodora: gift of God (Greek)

Theodosia: God given (Greek)

Theola: God's name is divine (Greek)

Theone: gifts of God (Greek)

Theora: watchful (Greek)

Thera: wild (Greek)

Thora: thunder (Scandinavian)

Thyra: dedicated to the god of war (Norse); shield bearer (Greek)

Tia: deer (Tongan); fairy queen (Russian)

Tiana: graceful princess (Hebrew)

Tiara: jewel crown (Latin)

Tida: daughter (Thai)

Tierney: grandchild or the chief (Irish)

Tifara: happy (Hebrew)

Tiffany: revelation of God, God appears to her (Greek)

Tiki: green stone, powering (Maori)

Tilda: powerful warrior (German); strength through the battle (German)

Tilly: fortunate warrior (Greek)

Timi: she honors God (English)

Tomone: listening (Hebrew)

Timothea: one who honors God (Greek); little (English)

Tina: Christian (Latin); enclosure (Hebrew)

Tira: arrow (Hindi)

Tish: happy (English)

Tisha: happy (English)

Titania: graceful great one, giant (Greek)

Titia: giants, great size and power (Greek)

Tiulpe: jewel flower (Tongan)

Tivona: fondness for nature (Hebrew)

Tobi: God is good (Hebrew)

Tobia: God is good (Hebrew)

Tocarra: dearest friend (Irish)

Tohuia: flower (Polynesian)

Toinette: priceless (Greek)

Tokoni: helper (Tongan)

Tola: flowering (Polish)

Tolla: priceless (Polish)

Toloa: Southern Cross constellation (Tongan)

Tomi: wealthy (Japanese)

Toni: priceless (Greek)

Tonia: priceless (Greek)

Tonneli: priceless Swiss

Tora: tiger (Japanese)

Tori: bird of victory (Japanese)

Torianna: graceful (Latin)

Toshi: mirror reflection (Japanese)

Totti: baby, little one (English)

Tovah: good (Hebrew)

Toya: door that leads into a valley (Japanese)

Toyah: door that leads into a valley (Japanese); warrior (Gaelic); late Summer (Greek)

Tracey: courageous (Latin); warrior (Gaelic); late Summer (Greek)

Tracie: courageous (Latin); warrior (Gaelic); late Summer (Greek)

Tracy: courageous (Latin)

Treasure: precious (English)

Treveen: cautious one, large village house (Welsh)

Trevina: from the homestead (Welsh)

Triana: graceful third born child (Latin)

Trina: purity (Scandinavian)

Trinity: three, father the son and the holy ghost (Latin)

Trisha: noble (Latin)

Trista: sad (Latin)

Tristanne: graceful (Latin)

Tristabelle: beautiful (Latin); sorrowful (French)

Tristen: loud (Latin)

Trixi: voyager, blessed (Latin)

Trixie: voyager, blessed (Latin)

Truda: strong spear (German)

Trudy: strong spear (German)

Tsomah: fair haired (Native American)

Tsula: fox (Native American); leaping water (Native American)

Tula: peace (Hindi)

Tullia: peaceful (Irish)

Tulsi: basil herb (Hindi)

Tuwa: earth (Native American)

Tyanna: graceful (Latin)

Tyler: tile layer (English)

Tyne: river (English)

Tyra: warrior (Scandinavian)

U

Ualani: heavenly rain (Hawaiian)

Ualusi: walrus (Tongan)

Uchenna: God's will (African)

Uda: prosperous, wealthy (English)

Udele: prosperous, wealthy (English)

Udiya: God's fire (Hebrew)

Uha: rain (Tongan)

Uha-tea: sun shower (Tongan)

Uhila: lightning (Tongan)

Ujana: noble excellence (African); jewel of the sea (Celtic); wealthy (Spanish)

Ula: inheritor (German)

Ulalia: speaks sweetly (Greek)

Ulani: light hearted, cheerful (Hawaiian)

Ulema: wisdom (Arabic); wilful (German)

Ulla: to fill (French)

Ulu: second born child (African)

Ululani: heavenly inspiration (Hawaiian); nation (Hebrew); peace (Sanskrit)

Uma: mother, flax (Hindi)

Umali: generous (Hindi)

Umayma: little mother (Arabic)

Umina: sleeping child (Aboriginal)

Umniya: desired (Arabic); one (Latin)

Una: lamb (Irish)

Unity: together (English)

Unna: woman (Icelandic)

Unnea: linden tree (Norse)

Uri: God's light (Hebrew)

Urianna: heaven (Greek)

Ursa: little bear (Greek)

Ursula: little she bear (Latin)

Usha: sunrise (Sanskrit)

Utano: song field (Japanese)

Utina: woman of my country (Native American)

V

Vail: from the valley (English)

Vailea: talking water (Polynesian); singled out (German)

Val: strength (Latin)

Vala: chosen (German)

Valancia: strength (Latin); renowned ruler (German)

Valda: hero ruler of the battle (Norse)

Valencia: strong, brave (Spanish)

Valene: strength (Latin)

Valentia: strong princess (Latin)

Valentina: strong, brave, healthy (Latin)

Valentine: strong, brave, healthy (Latin)

Valerie: strong, brave, healthy (Latin)

Valeska: powerful princess (Polish)

Valli: strength (Latin)

Vallia: powerful protector (Spanish)

Valonia: strong, brave (Latin)

Valora: brave, courageous, strong (Latin); golden Cambodian

Vana: sea urchin (Polynesian)

Vanaja: daughter from the forest (Hindi)

Vanda: stem (German)

Vandani: honorable (Hindi)

Vanessa: butterfly (Greek)

Vanetta: butterfly, golden (Greek)

Vani: voice (Hindi)

Vania: God is gracious (Hebrew)

Vanity: vain (English)

Vanja: God is gracious (Scandinavian)

Vanka: graceful (Russian)

Vanna: high (English)

Vanni: graceful (Italian)

Vanora: white wave (Welsh)

Vantrice: from the harvest (Greek)

Vanya: graceful (Russian)

Vara: cautious (Norse)

Varana: river (Hindi)

Varda: rose (Arabic)

Vardina: rose (Arabic)

Vardis: rose (Arabic); thorn (English)

Varina: stranger (Russian)

Varsha: rain (Hindi)

Vasanta: born at springtime (Sanskrit)

Vashti: very beautiful (Persian)

Vassy: most beautiful (Persian)

Veanna: graceful (Hebrew)

Veda: wisdom (Sanskrit)

Vedette: guardian (French)

Veera: strength (Hindi)

Vega: falling star (Arabic)

Vegena: feminine (Hawaiian)

Vehka: great glory (Bulgarian)

Vela: star constellation (Latin)

Velda: open field (German)

Veleda: wisdom (German)

Velika: great wisdom (Slavic); sweet like honey (Latin)

Velinda: gentle (Greek)

Viliya: great (Slavic)

Vellamo: rocking motion (Finnish)

Velma: determined, wilful (German)

Venus: goddess of love and beauty (Latin)

Vera: faithful, loyal (Russian); truth (Latin)

Verda: fresh (Latin)

Verdi: green like springtime (Latin)

Verdiana: truth is gracious, gracious green springtime (Latin)

Verena: possessor of sacred wisdom (Swiss); truth (Latin)

Verene: possessor of sacred wisdom (Swiss)

Verina: faithful (Latin)

Verita: truthful (Italian)

Verity: truthful (Italian)

Verona: truthful (Italian)

Verna: spring like (Latin)

Vernice: warrior (Latin)

Veronica: truthful, true image (Latin)

Vespera: evening star (Latin)

Vestah: star (Latin)

Veta: holy, sacred to God (Slavic)

Vevetta: white wave, fair haired (French)

Vevette: white wave, fair haired (French)

Vevina: sweet lady (Gaelic)

Vianca: white (Spanish)

Vianna: graceful violet flower (French)

Vianne: graceful violet flower (French)

Vica: life (Hungarian)

Vicki: victory (Latin)

Vicky: victory (Latin)

Victoria: victory (Latin)

Vida: beloved (Hebrew)

Vidonia: vine branch (Portuguese)

Vienna: graceful, capital of Austria (Latin)

Vija: wreath of flowers (Latvian)

Vika: victory (Polynesian)

Vila: dweller in the country house (Latin)

Vilhelmina: determined, wilful, protection (German)

Vilhelmine: determined, wilful, protection (German)

Villette: small town (French); protecting guardian (Russian)

Vilma: wilful (Dutch)

Vina: vineyard (Spanish)

Vincentia: prevailing (Latin)

Vincenza: prevailing (Latin)

Vincenzia: prevailing (Latin)

Vinia: grapes, wine (Latin)

Vinita: vineyard (Spanish)

Vinna: from the vine (Spanish); musical instrument (Italian)

Viola: violet color or flower (Latin)

Violanie: violet color or flower (Latin)

Violante: violet color or flower (Latin)

Violet: violet color or flower (Latin)

Violetta: violet color or flower (Latin); closed (German)

Vira: blonde haired (Spanish)

Virginia: purity (Latin)

Virtue: purity (Latin)

Vittoria: victory (Italian)

Vivian: full of life (Latin)

Vixen: female fox (Latin)

Vjera: faith (Russian)

Voila: behold (French)

Voleta: flowing veil (French)

Vonda: one who is admired (Irish)

Vondra: brave, courageous (Slavic)

Vonna: archer (French)

Vonny: archer (French)

Vreneli: truthful, like her mother (German)

Vrida: green (Spanish)

Vye: wisdom (African)

Vyoma: sky (Hindi)

W

Wahalla: immortal (Norse)

Wahkuna: wood of arrows (Native American)

Waida: warrior (German)

Waikiki: stream from which water gushes (Hawaiian)

Wainani: beautiful water (Hawaiian)

Wakanda: magic power (Native American)

Wakenda: to waken (Norse)

Walaniki: true image (Hawaiian)

Waleria: brave, strong (Polish); tribe of the Vandals (Slavic)

Wanda: wanderer (German); pale skinned (English)

Waneta: a horse that rides into battle (Native American)

Wanika: God is gracious (Hebrew)

Wannetta: little pale one (English)

Wapeka: weapon used for protection (Norse)

Waratah: red flowering tree (Aboriginal)

Warda: guardian (German)

Washi: eagle (Japanese)

Wasila: healthy (English)

Wenda: white skinned (Welsh); friend (English)

Wendy: white (Welsh)

Wera: truthful (Polish)

Weslea: from the westerly meadow (English)

Whaley: belonging to the whale meadow (English)

Whitley: from the white meadow (English)

Whitney: white water (English)

Wikolia: victory (Hawaiian)

Wila: faithful (Hawaiian)

Wilda: untamed (English)

Wileen: determined guardian, protection (German)

Willa: determined guardian, protection (German)

Willow: willow tree (English)

Wilma: determined guardian, protection (German)

Wilona: resolute guardian (German)

Winda: hunter (Swahili)

Winema: woman chief (Native American)

Winna: friends (African)

Winnie: peaceful (English)

Winola: gracious (German)

Winona: first born daughter (Native American)

Winter: born during the winter time (English); closed (German)

Wira: blonde haired (Polish)

Wisia: victory (Polish)

Wrena: wren bird (English)

Wynne: fair haired (Celtic)

Wyuna: clear water (Aboriginal)

X

Xana: blonde (Greek)

Xandi: defender of humankind (Greek)

Xandra: defender of humankind (Greek)

Xanthia: blonde (Greek)

Xanthis: blonde (Latin)

Xara: princess (Hebrew)

Xaveria: bright (Aramaic); owner of the new house (Spanish)

Xaviera: bright, brilliant (Arabic)

Xela: from the mountain (French)

Xena: welcomed, guest (Greek)

Xenia: hospitable (Greek)

Xerena: tranquil (Latin)

Xirena: alluring, siren (Greek)

Xuxa: lily (Brazilian)

Xyleena: from the forest (Greek)

Xylia: from the forest (Greek)

Xylina: from the forest (Greek)

Xylona: from the forest (Greek)

Y

Yaara: honey (Hebrew)

Yachne: hospitable (Hebrew)

Yael: mountain goat (Hebrew)

Yakira: precious (Hebrew)

Yalande: violet flower, purple (Greek)

Yalena: shining light (Russian)

Yalika: flowers of spring (Native American)

Yamelia: hard-working (German)

Yamilla: merchant (Slavic)

Yaminah: right, proper (Arabic)

Yamini: night time (Hindi)

Yamuna: sacred river (Hindi)

Yana: God is gracious (Slavic)

Yani: peaceful (Aboriginal)

Yara: seagull (Aboriginal)

Yarna: seagull (Aboriginal)

Yaralla: camping area (Aboriginal)

Yardena: descended (Hebrew)

Yarmilla: trader (Slavic)

Yarra: fast (Aboriginal)

Yashna: prayer (Hindi)

Yasmine: jasmine flower (Arabic)

Yatva: good (Hebrew)

Yedda: singer (English)

Yedida: dearest (Hebrew)

Yeira: light (Hebrew); shining light, sun ray (Russian)

Yelena: lily blossom (Latin)

Yelenah: shining light (Russian)

Yelisabeta: holy and sacred to god (Russian)

Yemena: from Yemen (Arabic)

Yemina: little dove (Hebrew)

Yenene: medicine woman (Native American)

Yesenia: flower (Latin)

Yeshara: direct (Hebrew)

Yeshisha: old (Hebrew)

Yesima: strength of right-hand (Hebrew)

Yessica: wealthy (Hebrew)

Yetta: ruler of the house (English)

Yevgenia: noble (Russian)

Yiesha: woman (Arabic)

Yola: violet flower, purple (Greek)

Yolanda: violet flower, purple (Greek)

Yoni: dove (Hebrew)

Yonina: dove (Hebrew)

Yonita: dove (Hebrew)

Yordana: descended (African)

Yoshe: lovely (Japanese)

Yoshi: quiet, respected (Japanese)

Yovela: happiness (Hebrew)

Ysabel: dedicated to God (Spanish)

Yuana: God is gracious (Spanish)

Yudelle: prosperous (English)

Yudita: praised (Russian)

Yula: young, youthful (Russian)

Yulene: youthful (Latin)

Yulia: youthful (Russian)

Yusra: wealthy (Arabic)

Yvanna: God is gracious (Slavic)

Yvette: young archer (French)

Yvonne: archer (French); seventh daughter (Hebrew)

Z

Zabrina: boundary (English)

Zada: lucky (Arabic)

Zafina: triumph (Arabic)

Zahara: flower (African)

Zahira: bright (Arabic); princess (Hebrew)

Zahra: flower (Swahili)

Zaida: good fortune (Arabic)

Zaidee: wealthy (Arabic); princess (Irish)

Zaira: dawn (Arabic); purity (Arabic)

Zakia: intelligent (Swahili)

Zakiya: purity (Swahili)

Zali: princess (Hebrew)

Zana: woman (Persian)

Zandra: defender of humankind (Greek)

Zaneta: with the grace of God (Hebrew)

Zanna: God is gracious (Spanish)

Zara: dawning brightness, radiance (Arabic)

Zarina: gold, golden (Hindi)

Zasha: defender of humankind (African)

Zaviera: bright (Spanish)

Zdena: follower of Dionysos (Greek)

Zehara: light (Hebrew)

Zelda: dark battle (German)

Zelene: sunshine (English)

Zelia: enthusiastic (Greek)

Zemira: song (Hebrew); woman (Persian)

Zena: guest (Greek)

Zenanda: queen (Persian)

Zenda: feminine (Persian)

Zenia: enthusiastic guest (Greek)

Zephira: morning (Hebrew)

Zera: seeds (Latin)

Zeta: olive (Hebrew); wolf (Hebrew)

Zeva: sword (Greek)

Zevida: gift (Hebrew)

Zigana: gypsy (Hungarian)

Zillah: shadow (Hebrew)

Zilya: harvester (Russian)

Zina: abundant (Hebrew); intriguing (Irish); hope (Latin)

Zita: little rose (Spanish)

Zizi: shining light (Hebrew)

Zoe: life (Greek)

Zofia: wisdom (Slavic)

Zohar: brilliant (Hebrew)

Zohra: blossom (Arabic)

Zoia: life (Russian)

Zolah: mound of earth (Italian)

Zona: girdle (Greek)

Zophie: wisdom Bohemian

Zora: dawn (Slavic)

Zorina: gold (Slavic)

Zosa: lily (Swiss)

Zoya: life (Slavic)

Zulema: peace (Hebrew)

Zurafa: lovely (Arabic)

Zuri: beautiful (Swahili)

Zusa: lily (Slavic)

Zwetlana: star (Russian)

SORTED BY MEANING A – Z

1 - 10

1000 generations: Chiyo (Japanese)
10th: Dixie (French)
10th born child: Dixie (French)

A

a gift: Darielle (French)

a horse that rides into battle: Waneta (Native American)

a sweet smelling plant: Marjolaine (French)

abundant: Zina (Hebrew)

accomplished: Seiko (Japanese)

accustomed: Solita (Latin)

active: Kineta (Greek)

admirable: Shae, Shay, Shea (Gaelic)

admired: Jodi, Jodie, Jody (Hebrew), Shavonda, Siobhain (Irish)

adorable: Adora (Latin), Cailida (Spanish), Endora (Hebrew)

adored: Adorlee (Greek), Isadora (English), Keiko (Japanese)

adventurous: Faren (English)

advice: Moina, Mona (Latin)

adviser: Monica (Latin), Reade (English)

adviser or divine counsellor: Alura (English)

advisor: Monique (Latin)

affection: Kerensa (English)

affectionate: Karenza (English), Mahalia (Hebrew), Minna (German), Morna (Gaelic), Rui (Japanese)

afflicted: Joby (Hebrew)

aflame: Celosia (Greek)

African skirt: Dashiki (Swahili)

alert: Casey (Gaelic), Kacie (Irish)

Alice's son: Alison (Irish), Allison (Irish)

alive: Bibiana (Latin)

alive and well: Aisha, Asha, Niesha (Arabic)

all gifts: Pandora (Greek)

all gods: Panthea (Greek)

alluring: Laka (Hawaiian), Sibena, Xirena (Greek)

alluring one: Cryena (Greek), Lori, Luraline, Lurline (German), Loriann (English)

alluring siren: Sirena (Greek)

alone: Aleena (Dutch), Solange (Latin)

always flowering: Aiyana (Native American)

ambition: Meta (Latin)

ambitious: Almeta, Almita (Latin)

amen: Emeni (Tongan)

ancestral relic: Ola (Scandinavian)

ancient: Ciannait, Cien (Irish), Priscilla (Latin), Shannon (Gaelic)

angel: Angel, Angelina, Angeline, Engel, Engelina, Evangelina, Tangia (Greek), Anela, Arella, Erela (Hebrew), Kannitha (Cambodian)

angel of newborn babies: Kamili (Zimbabwean)

angelic: Heavenly (English)

animal horn: Keren (Hebrew)

anointed: Kirsten, Kirstie (Scottish)

anointed with oil: Levani, (Fijian)

apple tree: Bel (Hindi)

apricot: Morela, (Polish)

April: April (Latin)

archer: Evonne, Vonna, Vonny, Yvonne (French)

archer from the pool: Joyln (English)

ardent: Calida (Spanish), Rheta (Welsh)

aristocratic: Moina (Irish), Mona (Irish)

armor: Loric (Latin)

armored warrior: Bruna (German)

aromatic oil: Melita (Greek)

aromatic spice: Clove (Latin)

arrogant: Leiko (Japanese)

arrow: Siham (Arabic), Tira (Hindi)

artichoke: Cynara (Greek)

ascending or rising: Aaliyah, Aleah, Aliya (Hebrew)

ash tree: Ash (English)

ash tree meadow: Ashley (English)

asked for: Arabella (Latin), Sam, Samala, Sami, Samuela, Saula (Hebrew), Suma (Tanzanian)

aspen tree: Aspen (English)

attached: Levia (Hebrew)

attendant: Paige (English)

attractive: Adonia (Greek), Bonne, Bonnie (Scottish), Delwyn (Welsh), Delyth (Welsh), Lole (Tongan), Shalana (Irish)

aurora: Rori (Latin)

Autumn: Aki (Japanese), Autumn (Latin)

avocado: Avoka (Tongan)

B

baby: Totti (English)

baby deer: Fawn (French)

baby's nurse: Farrah (Arabic)

bailiff: Bailey (French)

bald: Calvina (Latin)

ball: Mari (Japanese)

ballet dancer: Lakalka (Tongan)

bamboo: Takeko (Japanese)

banana: Fusi, (Polynesian)

barren: Mahala (Hebrew)

basil herb: Tulsi (Hindi)

battle prepared warrior: Shammara (Arabic)

battle ready warrior: Shamara (Arabic)

battle stronghold: Hilda (German)

bay: Morie (Japanese)

bear: Nita (North American), Shanita (Native American)

bear yawning: Hausu (Native American)

beat: Cadence (Latin)

beat of my heart: Cushla (Irish)

beautiful: Adora, Arabella, Claribell, Melinda, Mira, Mirabel, Tristabelle (Latin), Aglaia, Bellanca, Calla, Callie, Callista, Jacy, Jacinda, Kaliope, Kallista (Greek), Alanis, Keely (Irish), Alina (Slavic), Amelinda, Belina, Clarinda, Jezebel, Linda, Lindie (Spanish), Ani, Kanani (Hawaiian), Bel, Belda, Belle (French),

Belinda, Bella (Italian), Ceinlys, Kaina (Welsh), Cho, Jaehwa (Korean), Daila (Latvian), Dolly, Farrah, Fleta, Idabelle, Kenisha, Teagan, Tegan (English), Hasina, Zuri (Swahili), Hermosa (Spanish), Ilona (Hungarian), Jamelia, Jamila, Jarnila, Maysun, Numa, Ramona (Arabic), Mayoree (Thai), Mee (Chinese), Merinda (Aboriginal), Nava, Shaina, Shaine, Shanie (Hebrew), Shameena (Hindi), Olanthe (Native American)

beautiful child: Adama (African), Maciko (Japanese)

beautiful christian: Christabel (Latin)

beautiful daughter of the hero: Igna, Ingrid (Scandinavian)

beautiful eyes: Shahla, Afghani, ,

beautiful flower: Ayanna (Swahili), Calantha (Greek), Camelia (Latin), Sumalee (Thai)

beautiful gift: Dorabella, Dorinda, Corabelle, Lidia (Greek), Jedda (Aboriginal)

beautiful jade stone: Lin (Chinese)

beautiful lily: Lilybelle (English)

beautiful meadow: Hialeah (North American)

beautiful one from the fairy palace: Shayna (Yiddish)

beautiful one sent from heaven: Noelani (Hawaiian)

beautiful rose: Rosabelle (Latin)

beautiful song: Melosa (Spanish)

beautiful trial: Sumiko (Japanese)

beautiful victory: Sigrid (Norse)

beautiful vine: Lata (Hindi)

beautiful water: Talise (Native American), Wainani (Hawaiian)

beautiful woman: Adorna (Greek), Annabelle (French), Belina (German)

beautiful young girl: Adara (Greek)

beautifully dressed : Alida (Greek)

beauty: Cosima (Greek), Hadara (Hebrew)

beaver: Tayanita (Native American)

beaver stream or meadow: Beverly (English)

bee: Debbie, Deborah, Debra (Hebrew)

before: Deja (French)

beginning: Nyssa (Greek)

beginning of the season: Kia, Shakeia, Shakia (African)

behaved: Sunita (Hindi)

behold: Voila (French)

behold - a daughter: Reubena (Hebrew)

belief: Nori (Japanese)

believer: Iman (Arabic), Raissa (French)

belonging to God: Nikah, Shanika (Russian)

belonging to the meadow of shells: Shelley (English)

belonging to the night: Lilith (Arabic)

belonging to the whale meadow: Whaley (English)

beloved: Amelinda (Spanish), Carissa (Greek), Caryl (Welsh), Daralis (English), Davida, Davita, Didi, Vida (Hebrew), Davonna (Scottish), Kalia (Arabic), Lamorna, Shrai, Sherissa, Sherita (French), Sheryl (Welsh), Suki (Japanese)

beloved cherry tree: Cherie (French)

beloved from the pool: Darrelyn (English)

beloved lily: Susammi (French)

beloved one from the meadow: Leeba, Yiddish

beloved warrior: Gerda (German)

bend in the river: Miandetta (Aboriginal)

beneficent: Amethyst (Greek)

berry: Aerona (Welsh), Berry (English)

berry clearing: Bailey (English)

best: Areta, Aretha, Retha (Greek)

best friend: Safiya (Arabic)

better: Meliora (Latin)

bird: Avis (Latin), Cholena, Sakuna (Native American), Derora (Greek), Deryn (Welsh), Eca (Nigerian), Feige (Hebrew), Kula, Liliko (Tongan)

bird flying: Tashi (Native American)

bird of peace: Dove (English)

bird of prey: Daya (Hebrew)

bird of victory: Tori (Japanese)

bird with bright feathers: Lourie (African)

birdlike: Ava, Avice (Latin)

birthday: Latasha, American, Natasha (Latin), Tasaria (Russian)

bitter: Leire, Mairi, Miri, Miriam (Hebrew), Macia, Manka, Marjan (Polish), Maire (Irish), Manette (Latin), Manon (French), Manya (Russian)

bitter: Marabel (English), Marfa (Latin), Marja (Finnish), Maroula (Greek), Maruca, Marushka (Spanish), Mhairie (Scottish), Moira (Gaelic)

black: Ciara, Sierra (Irish), Ebony, Raven (English), Eponi, Siete (Tongan), Kala (Hindi), Kali (Sanskrit), Kara (Turkish), Kerrianne (Celtic), Nerina, Nigella (Latin)

black cockatoo: Beela (Aboriginal)

black duck: Mara (Aboriginal)

black eyes: Eleele (Hawaiian)

black fox: Inola, (North American)

black haired: Raven (English)

black wood: Ebony (English)

blackbird: Meriel (Hebrew), Merie (French), Meryl (Irish),

blessed: Beata, Benita, Grace, Gracia, Trixi, Trixie (Latin),

Chikri (Swahili), Delwyn, Gwen, Gwenda (Welsh), Maritza, Martiza, Nima (Arabic)

blessed happiness: Surata, (Pakistani)

blessed ring: Gwendolyn (Welsh)

blessing: Branda (Hebrew), Gratiana (Latin)

blind: Cecilia, Cicely, Secelia, Seelia (Latin), Cissy (Welsh)

blissful: Elysia (Latin)

blonde: Bellanca, Xana, Xanthia (Greek), Blanca (Spanish), Elivira, Oriole, Xanthis (Latin)

blonde haired: Vira (Spanish), Wira (Polish)

blooming: Floria, Florie (Latin),

blooming flower: Blossom (English)

blooming meadow: Ardelia, Ardella (Hebrew)

blossom: Zohra (Arabic)

blossom flower: Hana (Japanese)

blossoming flowers: Florine (Latin)

blue: Safaia (Tongan), Sapphire, Sapphira (Greek)

blue bird: Doli (Native American)

blue crested bird: Jaylene, Jay (Latin)

blue lapis: Azura (Persian)

blue sky: Larmina (Persian), Sky (English)

blueberry: Mora (Spanish)

boar battle: Averil (English)

boar friend: Orwin (Hebrew)

boar warrior woman: Avril (English)

body: Soma (Greek)

bold: Conradine, Lenice (German)

boomerang: Kylie (Aboriginal)

born after twins: Kissa, (Ugandan)

born at Christmas time: Noeline (Latin)

born at dawn: Cho (Japanese)

born at Easter time: Pascale (French)

born at springtime: Vasanta (Sanskrit)

born by the sea: Nenet (Egyptian)

born during summer: Summer (English)

born during the autumn rain: Jora (Hebrew)

born during the day: Dae (English)

born during the month of May: May (Latin)

born during the night: Sayo (Japanese)

born during the ninth month of the Jewish year: Sivanah, (Israeli)

born during the winter time: Winter (English)

born in April: April (Latin), Avril (English)

born in June: June (Latin)

born in the morning: Asa (Japanese)

born of a joyous father: Gail (Hebrew)

born of the ferries: Perizada (Persian)

born on a moonlit night: Shahar (Arabic)

born on a Saturday: Ama, Ghanaian, Sanya (Sanskrit)

born on Christmas day: Latasha, Natalie, Tasha (Latin), Natasha (Russian), Tasma (Slavic)

born on Friday: Efia (African)

born on January 6: Epiphany (Hebrew)

born on Sunday: Esi, (Ghanaian)

born on Thursday: Lakya (Hindi)

born on Tuesday: Abena (Ghanaian)

born under the sign of Aries: Lamesha, Tamesha (Hindi)

born under the sign of Aries: Mesha (Latin)

born under the sign of Pisces: Larmina (Hindi)

borrowed: Saula (Hebrew)

bound: Beca, Becky (Slavic), Reba, Rebecca (Hebrew)

bound together: Tais (Greek)

boundary: Brina, Bryn, Sabrina (Latin) , Zabrina (English)

bounded: Leanna, Leanne (French),

bountiful: Idelle (Celtic), Pepita (Spanish)

bow: Poloma (Native American),

braid: Kumi (Japanese)

brandy: Brandy (Dutch)

brave: Abira (Hebrew), Andria, Andriana, Valentina, Valentine, Valerie, Valonia, Valora (Latin), Casey, Keena (Irish), Deandra (French), Ebba (Norse), Valencia (Spanish), Vondra (Slavic), Waleria (Polish)

brave lioness: Liviya (Hebrew)

brave ruler: Erica (English)

brave spear carrier: Geraldine, Geri, Jeraldine, Jeri (German)

brave spear carrier from the pool: Jerilyn (German)

brave strength: Rita (Hindi)

brave woman: Ondrea (Slavic)

breath: Andra (Norse)

breeze: Lera (Russian)

bride: Beulah (Hebrew)

bridge: Cantara (Arabic)

bright: Alaina (Celtic), Alba, Bertha, Sunny (English), Alina (Slavic), Ally, Bobbi (German), Bela (Hungarian), Ceara, Claribell, Clarinda, Clarissa, Clarita (Latin), Chiara, Febe (Italian), Elenola, Hoaka, Kalala, Kalea (Hawaiian), Elva, Elvie, Elvy (Irish), Fipe (Polynesian), Javiera, Zaviera (Spanish), Phoebe (Greek), Seiran (Welsh), Xaveria (Aramaic), Zahira

(Arabic)

bright child: Akiko (Japanese), Alanis (Irish)

bright day: Dana, Dayna (English)

bright fame: Roannah (German)

bright land: Lamia (German)

bright light: Leoma (English)

bright meadow and sunny clearing: Shirley (English)

brightly shining: Phedra (Greek)

brightness: Lopeka (Hawaiian)

brilliant: Claire, Clara, Clare (Latin), Clarinda (Spanish), Gigi (German), Zohar (Hebrew)

brilliant beauty: Aglaia (Greek)

bringer of bliss: Sachi (Japanese)

bringer of comfort: Salwa (Arabic)

bringer of happiness: Ahyoka (Native American), Bliss (English)

bringer of light: Luca (Italian), Lucia, Lucinda, Lucindee (Latin), Lucille (English)

brings happiness to the earth: Kishi (Japanese)

brings joy and happiness: Bea, Beatrice (Latin)

brings rain: Ara (Arabic)

broken pot: Sutki (Native American)

brooding: Doreen (Irish)

brown hair: Aubery (French)

brown haired: Morena (Spanish)

brown hills: Kiona, Kiowa (Native American)

brown or red complexion: Caera (Irish)

brown skin: Bruna (Italian)

buffalo of the plains: Buffy (Native American)

burning: Ignacia (Latin)

burning flames: Blaise (English)

butterfly: Cho (Japanese), Danessa (Hebrew), Kimana (Native American), Kimimela (North American), Nessa (Norse), Pepe (Tongan), Phanessa, Vanessa, Vanetta (Greek)

C

call out: Kaila (Tongan)

calm: Galina (Greek), Mandara (Hindi), Sarila, Sarina, Serena, Serene, Serenity (Latin)

calm heavens: Nalani (Hawaiian)

calm heel: Galena (Greek)

camp: Ira (Aboriginal)

camping area: Yaralla (Aboriginal)

campsite: Noora (Aboriginal)

canal: Kanali (Tongan)

canary: Kaneli (Tongan)

canary yellow: Melina (Latin)

candle: Chandella (French)

candle holder: Menora (Hebrew)

candy: Lole (Tongan)

canopy: Marquita (French)

capital of Austria: Vienna (Latin)

capital of France: Paris (French)

caramel: Kalameli (Tongan)

care for: Cherish (English)

carefree: Calandra, Raine, Raisa (Greek)

caress: Haido (Greek), Lateefa (Arabic)

caring: Charity (Latin)

carried away: Takina (Tongan)

carrot: Kaloti (Tongan)

carry: Tara, Aramaic, ,

carved stone: Gisa (Hebrew)

cascade: Jirakee (Aboriginal)

cassia tree: Kassia, Kezia (Hebrew)

castle: Cala (Arabic)

castle on the rocky island: Carey (Welsh)

castor plant: Kiki (Egyptian)

cat like: Faline (Latin)

catcher: Rana (Scandinavian)

cautious: Pru, Prudence, Prue (Latin), Vara (Norse)

cautious one: Treveen (Welsh)

cedar tree: Ornice (Hebrew), Sita (Tongan)

celebration: Deni, Denise (French)

ceremony: Tana (Aboriginal)

champion: Neala, Tennille (Irish), Nigella (Gaelic)

chanting: Inoa (Hawaiian)

charitable: Charity (Latin), Shardae (Hindi)

charity: Carita (Latin)

charm: Charmaine (English)

charming: Lalita (Sanskrit)

cheeky: Sass (Irish)

cheerful: Blythe, Corliss (English), Hilary (Greek), Ulani (Hawaiian)

cheerful girl: Ailsa (German)

cherished: Cherise, Sherry (French), Cherish (English), Dee-Dee (Hebrew)

cherry: Cera (Irish), Cerise, Charrissee, Cherise, Sharice (French)

cherry blossom: Sakura (Japanese)

cherry fruit: Cherry (English), Cheryl (Welsh)

cherry tree: Nyora (Aboriginal)

chestnut: Kuri (Japanese)

chicken hawk: Liluye (Native American)

chief of the valley: Kendelle (Celtic)

chief of the valley of light: Kendellana (Greek)

chief who is noble and kind: Kimalina (Latin)

chief whose God is gracious: Kimanna (Hebrew)

chieftain: Melva, Melvina (Gaelic)

child: Keiki (Hawaiian), Moesha (Egyptian), Talitha, Tally (Hebrew)

child born after twins: Tawia (African)

child born at sunrise: Tasaria (Gypsy)

child born during the night: Layla, Leila (Swahili)

child born during the rainy season: Mashika (Swahili)

child born in happiness: Kioko (Japanese)

child born in prosperous times: Neema (Swahili)

child born on a Sunday: Cyriaca (Greek), Neda (Slavic), Sabbatha (Hebrew)

child born on Christmas day: Nitasha (Russian)

child born on Tuesday: Mardi (French)

child born under the sign of Capricorn: Makara (Hindi)

child of God: Sharik (African)

child of heavenly flowers: Leilani (Hawaiian)

child of purity: Makayla, Meka, Micah (Greek)

child of the handsome one: Mackenna (Gaelic)

child of water: Nirveli (Hindi)

child who lives long: Kameko (Japanese)

China: Kina (North American)

chosen: Elita (Latin), Vala (German)

chosen by God: Jeremia (Hebrew)

Christian: Chrissy, Christa, Christen, Christian, Christy, Tina (Latin), Chrys (English), Kristen (Scandinavian), Kristianna (Hebrew), Kristine (Danish), Stina (German)

Christmas: Noeline (French)

Christmas carol: Carol (English)

chrysanthemum flower: Kiku (Japanese)

cinnamon spice: Ketzia (Hebrew)

circle: Mariko (Japanese)

citizen: Quirita (Latin)

city: Medina (Arabic)

city fortification: Bailey (English)

clarity: Candice (Latin)

clay: Kele (Tongan)

clean: Fleta (English)

cleansed: Lavelle (Latin)

clear: Crystal, Krystal (Latin), Jala (Arabic), Kiyoka (Japanese)

clear mountain: Kelda (Scandinavian)

clear sky: Kasota (Native American)

clear water: Wyuna (Aboriginal)

clearing: Ainsley (English)

clever: Cassidy (Irish), Kassidy (Gaelic), Ludella (English)

climbing plant: Bryony (English)

closed: Elivira, Violetta, Winter (German)

cloth of fine linen: Sidba (Greek)

cloud: Mirrin (Aboriginal)

coastal shoreline: Ora (English)

cockatoo: Arora (Aboriginal)

coconut: Coco (Spanish)

comfort: Comfort (English)

comfort during a time of unhappiness: Solace (Latin)

comforting: Aza (Arabic)

companion: Ruta (Hebrew)

compassion: Leanore (Greek)

compassionate: Dara (Hebrew), Mercia, Mercy, Ruth (English)

complete: Irma (German), Japera (Zimbabwean)

concealed: Misty (English)

concealer: Lami (Tongan)

conception: Chita, Concha, Conchita (Latin)

confectionery: Candy (English)

confident: Rukan (Arabic)

confirmation: Avery (French)

conquer who is victorious: Sigourney (English)

conquering guardian: Signa (Norse)

consolation: Consuela, Suela (Spanish)

constant: Connie, Constance (Latin)

coral: Marjan (Persian)

cornell tree: Cornelia (Latin)

cottage: Bryony (German)

counsellor: Radella (English)

courageous: Andria, Andriana, Tracey, Tracie, Tracy, Valora (Latin), Vondra (Slavic), Carlotta (Italian), Charla (English), Charmaine (German), Riley, Rylee (Irish), Taddea, Tadia (Greek)

courageous one from the valley: Deandra (French)

courageous or strong: Carol, Corolann, Carolina, Caroline

(German)

covered in gold: Gilda (English)

covered in oil: Kirsten, Kirstie (Scottish)

covered in snow: Karli (Turkish)

covered with a mist: Misty (English)

covering the earth: Deita, Demi (Greek)

coyote chasing deer: Kaliska (Native American)

crash of thunder: Talma (Native American)

crayfish: Ingar (Aboriginal)

cream colored: Galatea (Greek)

creamy color: Ivory (English)

creating: Jivanta (Hindi)

creator: Nata (Native American)

crooked nose: Cami (Latin)

crow: Kalou (Tongan)

crown: Atara, Kayla, Liviya (Hebrew), Kalauni (Tongan), Taja (Sanskrit)

crown of laurel: Cayla, Kelila (Hebrew)

crown of laurel in the rain: Laraina, Laraine (English)

crown of laurel leaves: Lora, Loree, Lorelei, Loren, Lorena, Lorenza, Lori, Lorice, Lorina, Lorissa, Lorna (Latin), Loricia (Greek), Loris (Spanish)

crown of laurel leaves in the meadow: Caeley (Hebrew), Lorraine (English)

crowned: Cornona (Latin), Stefanida (Russian), Stefannia, Steffi, Stephanie, Stevana, Stevie (Greek)

crystal: Kalistala (Tongan), Ratana (Thai)

cultured: Alima (Arabic)

cup: Chalice (French)

curly hair: Cassidy (Irish)
curly haired: Cinnia (Latin)
curly head: Kassidy (Gaelic)
cut: Prisma (Greek)
cute: Gidget (English)

D

daffodil: Narcisse (French)

dahlia flower: Dahlia (English)

dairy queen: Tahnee (Russian)

daisy: Greta (English), Meagan, Megan, Peggy, Rissa (French)

daisy flower: Daisy (English)

dancer: Bina (Swahili), Nata (Sanskrit)

dancing: Mahola (Hebrew)

dancing bear: Sapata (Native American)

dark: Darcelle (Irish), Siete (Tongan)

dark battle: Griselda, Zelda (German)

dark blue: Indigo (Latin)

dark complexion: Darcy (Irish)

dark haired: Darcy, Kyrie (Irish), Kerry (Celtic), Laili (Arabic), Malania, Melanie (Greek), Maris, Maura, Morissa, Nigella (Latin), Maurise, Moriah (French), Mela (Polish)

dark haired graceful one: Kerrianne (Celtic)

dark lipped: Lamya (Arabic)

dark skinned: Maureen (French), Sauda (Swahili)

darkness before midnight: Lisha (Arabic)

darling: Darla, Darlene (English), Libusa (Slavic)

darting hummingbird: Litonya (Native American)

date fruit: Tamara, Thamar (Hebrew)

date palm: Tammy, Tamra (Hebrew)

daughter: Hika (Polynesian), Jama (Sanskrit), Natane (Native American), Tanay, Tanaya (Hindi), Tida (Thai)

daughter from the forest: Vanaja (Hindi)

daughter of heaven and earth: Dione (Greek)

daughter of Jehovah: Bethia (Hebrew)

daughter of oath: Bathsheba (Hebrew)

daughter of the Earth: Hermoine (Greek)

daughter of the prophet: Fatima (Arabic)

daughter of the wind god: Canace (Greek)

daughter whose father is difficult: Kesi (Swahili)

dawn: Alaula (Hawaiian), Ata (Tongan), Bara (Aboriginal), Dawn, Morna (English), Rokeya (Persian), Rori (Latin), Sahar, Zaira (Arabic), Zora (Slavic)

dawning: Ladawna (English)

dawning brightness: Zara (Arabic)

day: Dai (English)

daybreak: Dawn (English)

daylight: Minkie (Aboriginal)

day's eve: Daisy (English)

dear: Cher, Cherie, Cherilyn, Sheri (French), Cushla (Irish)

dearest: Tamila (Russian), Yedida (Hebrew)

dearest friend: Tocarra (Irish)

dearly loved friend: Caera (Latin)

decorated: Orna (Latin)

decorated with jewels: Adorna (Latin)

decoration: Adena (Hebrew)

dedicated to God: Belica, Isabella, Isabelle, Ysabel (Spanish)

dedicated to Mars: Marcella, Marcena, Marcia, Marcie (Latin)

dedicated to the god of war: Thyra (Norse)

deep snow: Miyuki (Japanese)

deep water: Binda (Aboriginal)

deer: Ayla, Sivia (Hebrew), Dyani (Native American), Tia (Tongan)

defender: Aminta (Greek), Brina (Slavic)

defender of human kind: Lysandra, Lexadra, Sacha (Greek), Sandra, Sandre, Sandy (English),Sasha, Shura (Russian), Zasha (African), Saundra, Shandra, Sondra, Xandi, Xandra, Zandra (Greek)

defender of man: Aleka, Alex, Alexandra, Alexis (Greek)

delicate: Adina (Hebrew), Maeve (Gaelic)

delicate fabric: Lacey (English)

delightful: Delicia, Happi (English), Maja, Majid (Arabic)

delivering: Lora, Loree, Lorelei (Latin)

dependent: Lia (Hebrew)

descended: Yardena (Hebrew), Yordana (African)

descending: Giordana (Italian), Jardena, Jordan (Hebrew)

desire: Hope (English), Desi (French), Edana (Celtic), Ehani (Hindi), Erasma (Greek)

desired: Onida (Native American), Umniya (Arabic)

destiny: Carma, Karma (Sanskrit)

determined: Velma, Vilhelmina, Vilhelmine (German)

determined guardian: Wileen, Willa, Wilma (German)

determined strength: Melisande (German)

devoted: Sadhana, Sadhana (Hindi)

devoted to God: Lemula (Greek)

devout: Pia (Italian)

dew: Rocio (Latin), Tali (Hebrew)

dew drop: Chunami, (North American)

dew of the sea: Rosemary (Latin)

diadem: Atara (Hebrew)

diamond: Kailmana (Hawaiian)

diamonds: Taimani (Tongan)

difference: Delta (Greek)

dignified: Jaha (Swahili), Solenne (French)

dimple: Fosetta (French)

direct: Yeshara (Hebrew)

discretion: Pru, Prudence, Prue (Latin)

distinctive air: Aura (Greek)

distinguished: Shalena (Norwegian)

distressed: Joby (Hebrew)

divine: Deana, Deandra, Deanna, Divinia (Latin), Guda (Scandinavian)

divine: Deva, Divya, Shakti (Hindi), Tecla, Thea (Greek), Diana, Diane, Ladivina (English)

divine announcement: Orela (Latin)

divine counsellor or adviser: Alura (English)

divine flower: Diantha (Greek)

divine gift: Fedora (Greek)

divine name: Theano (Greek)

divine protector: Osma (English)

divine strength: Astrid (Norse), Osita (Spanish)

divinely protected: Selima (Scandinavian)

doctor: Asa (Hebrew)

doe: Hinda (Hebrew), Rae (English), Taylor (Celtic)

doll like: Dolly (English)

dolphin: Delphine (Greek), Naia (Hawaiian)

donkey: Ona (Greek)

door that leads into a valley: Toya, Toyah (Japanese),

double canoe: Kalia (Tongan)

dove: Haiwee (Native American), Jonina, Yoni, Yonina, Yonita (Hebrew), Paloma (Spanish), Tauba (German)

doves of peace: Jemima (Hebrew)

dragon: Ryo (Japanese)

dream: Aissa (Gaelic), Maya (Hindi)

dreamer: Imena (African), Lotus (Greek)

dry earth: Azalea (Greek)

dry white wine: Chablis (French)

dweller from the farm near the woods: Shakela (Irish)

dweller in the country house: Vila (Latin)

dwelling: Shaleisha (Hebrew)

E

eager: Amalea (German), Ardis (Latin)

eagle: Arabella (German), Ava (Greek), Orell, Orlenda (Russian), Osyka (Native American), Washi (Japanese)

earth: Gaia (Greek), Tera (Latin), Tuwa (Native American)

earthly: Herma (Greek)

earthy: Teangi (Aboriginal), Terra (Latin)

easterly wind: Solana (Latin)

eastern: Anatolia (Greek)

eastern sky: Kaina (Hawaiian)

eastern wind: Solenne (Spanish)

ebony: Eponi (Tongan)

echo: Sawni (Native American)

egg: Ovia (Latin)

Egyptian goddess: Qadesh (Egyptian)

eight born child: Ottavia (Italian), Tavia (Latin)

eighth: Ottavia (Latin)

either: Kinta, (North American)

elder: Gamel (Scandinavian), Keshisha (Arabic)

eldest sister: Aneko (Japanese), Minya (Native American)

elegant: Sumi (Japanese)

elevated: Alta (Latin), Elata (Latin)

elf: Alva (Swedish), Alvina, Eletta, Elvie, Elvy (English), Aubery (German), Laella (French), Nissa (Scandinavian)

elf counsel: Avery (English)

embracing everything: Ima (German)

emerald: Esmeralda (Spanish), Meralda (Latin), Mya (Burmese), Ruri (Japanese)

enchantress: Ianira (Greek), Mohini (Sanskrit), Sidonia (Phoenician)

enclosure: Tina (Hebrew)

enduring: Patience (Latin)

energetic: Mehira (Hebrew)

energy: Mahira (Hebrew), Sakti (Hindi)

energy circle: Chaka, Chakra, Shakeena, Shakeia (Sanskrit)

enlightened: Aharona (Hebrew)

enlightened singing: Arnina (Hebrew)

entertainer: Samira (Arabic)

enthusiastic: Ardella (Latin), Rheta (Welsh), Zelia (Greek)

enthusiastic guest: Zenia (Greek)

essence: Quintessa (Latin)

eternal: Chiyo (Japanese), Melesse (Ethiopian)

eternal beauty: Amara (Latin)

eternal life: Athanasia (Greek)

eternal ruler: Elika (Hawaiian)

ethereal: Airlea (Greek)

Eucalyptus tree: Karri (Aboriginal)

evening: Jaamini, Rajani (Hindi)

evening time: Karrin (Aboriginal)

everlasting: Amara, Amarinda (Greek)

ewe: Rachelle, Raquel, Rachel (French), Rae (English)

exalted: Bria (Gaelic), Brianna, Brianne (Celtic), Brita, Britt, Britta (Norwegian), Elisha, Elli (German), Ilysa (Greek)

exalted nature: Heidi (German)

exalted one: Bedelia, Bridget (Gaelic)

excellence: Areta, Aretha (Greek)

excellent: Degula (Hebrew)

extend: Inge (English)

extreme: Maxine (Latin)

eye catching: Ramona (Arabic)

F

fair: Bronwyn, Eiddwen, Glenda, Gwen, Gwenda, Jenna (Welsh), Caley (Irish)

fair and smooth: Guinevere, Jennifer (Welsh),

fair friend: Eilwen (Greek)

fair hair: Fayre (English), Fenna (Norse)

fair haired: Alina, Ginnifer (Welsh), Aselma, Finola, Fiona (Gaelic), Bellanca (Greek), Blanche, Vevetta, Vevette (French), Eavan, Finna (Irish), Fair (English), Selma, Wynne (Celtic), Tsomah (Native American),

fair lady: Isolde (Welsh)

fair one from the pool: Gwendolyn (English)

fair rose: Roz (Spanish)

fair shoulders: Nuala (Irish)

fair speech: Lelia (Greek)

fair-haired: Oriole (Latin)

fairy: Fay (French), Feeli (Tongan), Nia (Irish)

fairy queen: Taneya, Tania, Tanya, Tanisha, Tata, Tatiana, Tia (Russian), Tannis (Slavic)

fairy queen found on Christmas day: Natania (Russian)

faith: Vjera (Russian)

faithful: Armine (Hebrew)

faithful: Beca, Becky (Slavic), Eiddwen (Welsh), Fealty, Leala (French), Vera (Russian), Wila (Hawaiian), Fidelity, Leandra, Verina (Latin), Reba, Rebecca (Hebrew)

faithful defence: Minette (French)

falcon: Shahina (Arabic), Takenya (Native American)

fall: Autumn (Latin)

falling star: Vega (Arabic)

fame: Clarice (Latin)

family: Niree (Aboriginal), Sherika (Arabic)

famous: Alba, Almira, Bertha, Elmina, Luella (English), Shahira (Arabic), Shalena (Norwegian), Tecla (Greek), Ally, Bobbi, Emmylou, Meryl, Rue (German), Ceara, Claire, Clara, Clare, Clarinda, Clarissa, Clarita, Lara (Latin), Chiara (Italian), Cleone, Clymene (Greek), Kalauka, Lopeka (Hawaiian)

famous beauty: Clorinda (Persian)

famous friend: Marvina (French)

famous in war: Heloise (French)

famous prophet: Rosamond (German)

famous reputation: Fayme (French)

famous rule: Ronli, Rori (Irish)

famous warrior: Aloysia, Aloysia, Eloisa, Eloise, Lorraine, Lou, Louisa, Louise (German), Laraina, Laraine, Lois (Greek), Luisa (Spanish),

famous wolf: Rudi, Rudy (German),

fanciful: Capri, Caprice (Italian),

farmer: Georgene (English), Gina, Jina, Jorja (Greek), Jirina (Slavic), Georgia, Georgina, Georginne (Latin)

farmhouse near the stream: Kelby (English)

fast: Druella (Latin), Keena (Irish), Yarra (Aboriginal)

fast runner: Saranu (Sanskrit)

fate: Destiny (French), Karma (Sanskrit), Moira (Greek)

father the son and the holy ghost: Trinity (Latin)

father's joy: Abigail (Hebrew)

favor: Grace, Gracia, Gratiana (Latin)

favorite: Kariss, Karissa (Greek), Keisha (Swahili), Kesia (African)

favorite gift: Karisma (Greek)

fawn: Fawn (French), Orpah (Hebrew)

female deer: Hinda (Hebrew), Lahela (Hawaiian)

female fox: Vixen (Latin)

female warrior: Beda (English)

feminine: Cai (Vietnamese), Sheila (Australian), Vegena (Hawaiian), Zenda (Persian),

fertile plain: Shara (Hebrew)

fertility: Diana, Diane (Latin), Isis (Egyptian)

festivity: Galla (Latin), Gala (French)

field: Blair (Scottish)

field of flowers: Ardith (Latin)

field of oats: Avena (Latin)

fiery: Eithne (Celtic), Enya (Scottish), Fira (English), Kalla (Aboriginal), Neci (Hungarian), Flame, Ignacia, Ignia, Igiga (Latin), Pyrena (Greek), Flanna, Flannery (Irish)

fiery leader: Edris (Welsh)

fifth: Penthea (Greek)

fifth born child: Penthea (Greek), Quinta, Quintana, Quintina (Latin)

fig tree: Idra (Aramaic)

fine: Anala (Hindi), Gala (Italian)

fine lace: Chantilly (French)

fire: Aine (Irish), Jany (Hindi), Nadalia (Aboriginal), Oriel (German), Pyralis (Greek), Souzan (Persian)

fire place: Kira (Aboriginal), Oola (Aboriginal)

fire stoker: Brenda (English)

first born: Alula (Arabic)

first born daughter: Winona (Native American)

first light: Dawn (English)

first rose: Primrose (English)

first to dance: Ayita (Cherokee)

first-born child: Katina (Aboriginal), Megara (Greek)

first-born daughter: Dede (African), Mina (Native American)

fish: Telae (Tongan)

flame: Blaine (English), Kalama (Hawaiian), Rudi (German), Rudy (German)

flaming: Celosia (Greek)

flat land: Kalana (Tongan)

flat metal: Flannery (French)

flattering: Ilka (Scottish)

flax: Uma (Hindi)

flour: Merrina (Aboriginal)

flourishing: Thalia (Greek)

flower: Aster, Calantha, Evanthe, Peony (Greek), Anh (Vietnamese), Azalea (English), Bakula, Mehadi, Jula (Hindi), Elodie, Flora, Yesenia (Latin), Fleur (French), Cveta (Slavic), Ilima, Melia, Pua (Hawaiian), Jessenia (Arabic), Kalina (Polish), Linnea (Swedish), Patya (Aboriginal), Posala (Native American), Tohuia (Polynesian), Zahara (African), Zahra (Swahili)

flower bud: Meiko (Japanese)

flower child: Hanako (Japanese)

flower with yellow and red blossoms: Nurita (Hebrew)

flower wreath: Garland (French), Kalei (Hawaiian)

flowering: Aiyana (Native American), Chloe, Cyma, Talia, Thalia (Greek), Fisi (Polynesian), Cassia, Florence, Floria, Florie (Latin), Mohala (Hawaiian), Tola (Polish)

flowering bush: Siale (Tongan)

flowers: Floris (English)

flowers of spring: Yalika (Native American)

flowery: Anthea (Greek)

flowing down: Jardena, Jordan (Hebrew),

flowing tide: Ebba (English)

flowing veil: Voleta (French)

flowing water: Saril (Turkish)

folding wings: Falda, Icelandic, ,

follower of Christ: Kirsten, Kirstie (Latin)

follower of Dionysius: Deni, Denise (French)

follower of Dionysos: Zdena (Greek)

follower of the prophet: Oma (Arabic)

following down: Giordana (Italian)

following secret: Runa (Norse)

fondness for nature: Tivona (Hebrew)

footloose: Eletta (Greek)

forgiving: Sameh (Arabic)

foreign woman: Bobbi (Latin)

foreign woman or stranger: Basia (Polish)

forest: Silika (Latin)

forever true: Faith (English)

forgetful: Letha (Greek)

forgive: Kai (Japanese)

fortress: Cala, Callie (Arabic)

fortunate: Felice, Feiica (Greek), Felicity (Latin), Fortuna, Fortune (Italian), Kichi (Japanese)

fortunate warrior: Tilly (Greek)

fortune: Kamata (Native American),

foundation of strength: Masada (Hebrew)

fountain of joy: Abigail (Hebrew)

four leaf clover: Clover (English)

fourth born child: Pita (Italian), Tess (Greek)

fourth born daughter: Delta (Greek)

fourth child: Tessa (Greek)

fourth letter of the alphabet: Delta (Greek)

fox: Tsula (Native American)

fragrant: Muriel (Greek)

fragrant flower: Jasmina, Jasmine (Persian)

free man: Carla, Carlene, Carlissa, Carlotta, Carly, Carol, Corolann, Carolina, Caroline, Carrie, Caryl, Chara, Charla, Charleen, Charlie, Charlotte, Karla, Karol, Karolina, Lotta, Lotte, Sharik (German), Sheri (French) ,

free to travel about: Aleta (Greek)

freedom: Cecania (German), Dinah (Hebrew), Frazea (Spanish), Liberty (Latin), Lysandra (Greek), Malaya (Filipino), Pancha (Spanish)

French: Francesca (Italian), Franci, Fronia (Latin), Francine (French)

fresh: Raanana (Hebrew), Verda (Latin)

fresh stream: Amaryllis (Greek)

friend: Carra (Irish), Dakota, Galilani (North American), Filia (Greek), Kora (Aboriginal), Raya, Ruta (Hebrew), Wenda (English)

friend to all: Alvina (English)

friend with a spear: Orva (French)

friendly: Amity (Latin), Anisah (Arabic), Damica (French), Ruta (Hawaiian)

friendly fairy: Niesha (Scandinavian), Nissa (Scandinavian)

friendly to all: Takota (Native American),

friends: Winna (African)

friendship: Amita, Ahuda (Hebrew)

frog: Ramona (Spanish)

from a chalk sea: Chelsea (English)

from brie in France: Brie (French)

from Britain: Bretta (Gaelic), Brita, Britt, Britta (English), Brittany (Irish)

from Chad: Chadee (French)

from China: Siana (Tongan)

from Delos: Delia (Greek)

from Delphi: Delphine (Greek)

from Denmark: Dana, Dayna (English)

from Edinburgh: Edina (English)

from France: Fran (Latin)

from Gaeta: Gaetana (Italian)

from Germany: Germaine, Jermaine (French)

from Hadria: Adria, Adriana, Adriane (Greek)

from India: India (Hindi)

from Ireland: Erin, Erinna (Celtic)

from Judea: Judith, Judy (Hebrew)

from Magdalen: Mada, Maddie, Madeleine, Madge (Hebrew)

from Milan: Mila (Italian)

from Mount Kynthos: Cindy (Greek)

from Persia: Persis (Greek)

from Rhodes: Rhodah (Greek)

from Rome: Roma, Romaine, Romana, Romilda, Romina (Roman)

from Sabines: Savina (Latin)

from the alder grove: Delany (French)

from the battleground: Garland (English)

from the beloved cool: Sherilyn (Celtic)

from the blessed isles: Elissa (Greek)

from the boundary line: Bree (Latin)

from the cape: Rossalyn (Scottish)

from the cherry tree near the pool: Cherilyn (Welsh)

from the coal pool: Colina (English)

from the court: Liss (Celtic)

from the crystal pool: Cyrstalin (Welsh)

from the dales or valley meadows: Dallas (Irish)

from the earth: Dhara (Hindi)

from the elder tree home: Nelda (English)

from the fairy palace: Breen (Irish), Shayla (Gaelic)

from the fairy palace in the meadow: Shaelea (Irish)

from the fairy palace pool: Shaelyn (Irish)

from the field: Felda (German)

from the forest: Sylwen (Latin), Xyleena, Xylia, Xylina, Xylona (Greek)

from the fortress: Darcelle (French)

from the fountain: Fontane (French), Fontanna (French)

from the fountain of youth: Endora (Hebrew)

from the graceful plains: Shareene (Hebrew)

from the hare meadow: Harlene (English), Harley (English)

from the harvest: Vantrice (Greek)

from the high tower: Leli (Swiss), Mada, Maddie, Madeleine, Madge (Greek)

from the hill of ore: Orell (English)

from the hollow: Corinne (French)

from the homestead: Trevina (Welsh)

from the house of God: Beth (Hebrew)

from the house of God's grace: Bethanny, (Aramaic)

from the house of gracious God: Jobeth (Hebrew)

from the house of mercy: Bethesda (Hebrew)

from the island: Lisle (English), Lyla (French)

from the jasmine flowers near the pool: Jazlyn (Persian)

from the land by the pool: Teralyn (Latin)

from the land of lakes: Lachianina (Scottish)

from the land with canyons: Nairi, (Armenian)

from the little road: Lanelle (French)

from the meadow: Aleah (English)

from the meadow clearing: Ainsley (English)

from the meadow strait: Kylie (Irish)

from the meadow with the tall trees: Taleah (English)

from the mill stream: Melba (Celtic)

from the moor: Maris, Morissa (Latin), Maurise (French)

from the mountain: Bryn (Welsh), Orea (Greek), Xela (French)

from the mountain valley: Corra (Irish)

from the Nile: Nila (Latin)

from the North: Narelle (Scandinavian), Norell (German)

from the open valley pool: Lindel (English)

from the peaceful rocky hill: Taryn (Irish)

from the place where the heather grows: Healther (English)

from the plains: Saronna, Sharna, Sharon (Hebrew)

from the pool: Meara (Gaelic)

from the pool in the meadow: Linleigh (English)

from the pool of life: Evelyn (Hebrew)

from the port of ships: Chelsea (English)

from the pure meadow: Caeley, Kalei, Kaylee (English)

from the pure pool: Cailin (Welsh), Caitlin (Irish)

from the Queen's lawn: Quintana (English)

from the riverbank: Riva, River (French)

from the rocky hill: Shantara, Shatara, Tari (Irish)

from the rose meadow: Rosalee, Rosalee (Latin)

from the rose pool: Rosita (English)

from the royal meadow: Kimberly (English), Rayleen (French)

from the sea: Coral, Maris (Latin), Delma (Spanish), Meredith (Welsh)

from the seaside: Elanora (Aboriginal)

from the shade pool: Shalyn (Welsh)

from the star meadow: Starlee (English)

from the star of the sea pool: Marilyn (Hebrew)

from the straight: Chanel (French)

from the stream: Brooke (English)

from the summer meadow: Suma (English)

from the tall meadow: Taylea (English)

from the town by the water: Portia (English)

from the valley: Dahila (Scandinavian), Douna (Slavic), Glenda (Irish)

from the valley: Dale, Denna, Lera, Vail (English)

from the vine: Vinna (Spanish)

from the westerly meadow: Weslea (English)

from the white meadow: Jenelia (Welsh), Whitley (English)

from the woods: Shakeita (Scottish)

from the yellow meadow: Fairlee (English)

from Wales: Cambria (Latin)

from where the roses grow: Rhodah (Greek)

from Yemen: Yemena (Arabic)

fruit: Carpathia (Greek)

fruit field: Carma (Arabic)

fruit harvest: Janaia, Janna (Arabic)

fruit which is sweet: Elma (Turkish)

fruitful: Efrata (Hebrew)

fruitful vineyard: Karmel (Hebrew)

full moon: Macalla (Aboriginal)

full of life: Vivian (Latin)

G

garden: Carmela, Carmen, Carmine, Gina (Hebrew)

garden of Lord: Ganya (Hebrew)

gardener: Malini (Hindi)

gazelle: Kapika (Hawaiian)

gazing: Raniyah (Arabic)

gem: Crystal (Greek), Gemma (Latin), Opal (Sanskrit), Ruby (French)

gem child of the Earth: Jemina, Czech, ,

gemstone: Azura (Persian)

generation: Dorita (Hebrew), Ede (Greek)

generation's beautiful child: Miyoko (Japanese)

generous: Hiriko (Japanese), Karima (Arabic), Lilo (Hawaiian), Macawi (Native American), Umali (Hindi)

gentle: Adina, Dalit (Hebrew), Blythe (English), Maru, Maru (Polynesian), Damaris, Malinda, Melinda, Mindy, Velinda (Greek), Halima (Swahili), Lateefa, Leftifa, Suhaila (Arabic)

gentle: Modesty (Latin), Morna (Gaelic), Myrna (Irish)

gentle breeze: Aura (Latin)

gentle deer: Shika (Japanese)

gentle dew drops from heaven: Tali (Hebrew)

gentle stream: Cari (Turkish)

giant: Titania (Greek)

giants: Titia (Greek)

giddy: Gidget (English)

gift: Daiya (Polish), Daryl (French), Daryn, Dora, Dore, Dorena, Doria, Doris, Dorothy, Dorothea, Dottie (Greek), Donata (Latin), Ebun (Nigerian), Lolotea (Spanish), Makana (Hawaiian), Teruma, Zevida (Hebrew)

gift from God: Doretta (Greek), Sheina (Hebrew), Dasha, Ladasha (Russian), Godiva (English)

gift of God: Derede, Dorita, Dorothy, Dorothea, Theodora (Greek), Mattea, Natania, Nathania, Shilo (Hebrew)

gift of Isis: Isadora (Latin)

gift of the sun: Elidi (Greek)

gifted ruler of the people: Derika (German)

gifts of God: Theone (Greek)

gilded: Doreen (French)

ginger: Imber (Polish)

ginger spice: Ginger (English)

girdle: Zona (Greek)

girl: Barite (Aboriginal), Cailin (Gaelic), Colleen (Irish), Hine (Polynesian), Ketina (Hebrew), Cora, Coreita, Cori, Corina, Corisande, Corissa, Kora (Greek), Kornina (English)

girl from the woods: Silvana (Italian), Silvia (Latin)

girl of my heart: Naarah (Hebrew)

girl who wears black: Chemarin (Hebrew)

giver of pleasure: Narmanda (Hindi)

giver of praise: Peony (Greek)

gives compliments: Blanda (Hebrew)

glad: Gai, Gay (French)

glenn: Glenna (Irish)

glorious: Gloria, Glorien, Glory (Latin), Hildemar (German), Kei (Hawaiian)

glorious calm: Keilana (Hawaiian)

glorious chief: Keilani (Hawaiian)

glorious ruler: Lada (Slavic)

glory: Cleone, Cleta, Clio (Greek), Gloria (Latin), Kololia (Tongan)

glory flower: Cleantha (Greek)

glory of the father: Cleopatra (Greek)

glowing: Ardelia, Candra (Latin), Candice, Dacia (Greek)

glowing with heat: Kahaka (Tongan)

goat: Aja (Hindi)

goblet: Chalice (French)

God blesses: Azariah (Hebrew)

God establishes: Joaquina (Hebrew)

God given: Theodosia (Greek)

God has added: Preilla (Spanish)

God has added a child: Fifi (French), Joline (Hebrew)

God has added a little child: Josetee, Josie (French)

God has answered: Eliana (Hebrew)

God has answered me: Iliana (Hebrew)

God has favored me: Chaanach, Chana, Hannah, Oni (Hebrew)

God has favored: Sheena, Shona, Sinead (Irish)

God has favored her: Rida (Arabic)

God has favored me: Ann, Anna, Anne, Anja, Annabella, Annabelle, Annetta, Annette, Annmarie (Hebrew)

God has given: Deodata (Greek)

God has healed: Rafaela, Raphaela (Hebrew)

God has spoken: Mireil (Hebrew)

God heard: Samantha (Hebrew)

God helps: Azariah (Hebrew)

God increases: Jolene (Hebrew)

God is a gracious: Joni (Hebrew)

God is good: Koana (Hawaiian), Tobi, Tobia (Hebrew)

God is gracious: Ana, Juana, Juanita, Yuana, Zanna (Spanish), Ania, Chana, Chenia, Gian, Ioana, Iva, Ivah, Ivanna, Jalena, Janae, Jane, Janie, Jayne, Janel, Janelle, Janet, Janice, Janika, Janine, Janique, Janita, Janna, Jasia, Jatara, Jayna, Jayne, Jean, Jo, Joan, Johanna, Johnna, Jontel, Kiannah, Kirianne, Lajuanna, Ohanna, Shana, Shanae, Shanice, Shanisa, Shauna, Shiona, Vania, Wanika (Hebrew), Gia, Giovanna (Italian), Jan, Jennica, Jonna (English), Jeanette, Jenelle (French), Seana, Shaunta, Shawna (Irish), Seini (Polynesian), Seona (Scottish), Vanja (Scandinavian), Yana, Yvanna (Slavic)

God is gracious and graceful: Joanna, Joanne (Hebrew)

God is gracious to her: Shawndelle (Irish)

God is listening: Samantha (Hebrew)

God is Lord: Ellice (Greek)

God is my crown: Katriel (Aboriginal)

God is my judge: Danessa, Daniah, Danice, Danielle, Danna, Dannal, Dani, Ranielle, Taniel (Hebrew)

God is my light: Eleora (Greek)

God is my oath: Bette, Betty, Ilsa, Isabella, Isabelle, Liese (Hebrew)

God is my salvation: Ikia (Hebrew)

God is my teacher: Mariah (Hebrew)

God is precious: Jana (Slavic)

God is willing: Joelle (Hebrew)

God is with us: Emmanuelle (Hebrew), Manuela (Spanish)

God listens: Ismaela (Hebrew)

god of healing: Peony (Greek)

god of the Earth: Malini (Hindi)

God of the wind: Anila (Hebrew)

God teaches: Jaira (Hebrew)

God will establish: Joakima (Hebrew)

God will help: Jususa (Hebrew)

God will increase: Josea, Josee (French), Josephine (Hebrew)

goddess: Asa (Norse), Dea (Latin), Rhiamon, Rhian (Welsh), Thea (Greek)

goddess gracious: Chavon (Hebrew), Hana (Hebrew), Jenice (Hebrew), Shinae (Irish)

goddess of agriculture: Chloe (Greek)

goddess of beauty: Lada (Russian)

goddess of dawn: Aurora (Greek)

goddess of fertility: Deita (Greek), Demi (Greek)

goddess of flowers: Feronia (African)

goddess of fruitfulness: Holla (German)

goddess of light: Tafne (Egyptian)

goddess of love: Aphrodite (Greek), Freya (Scandinavian), Tanith (Venetian)

goddess of love and beauty: Venus (Latin)

goddess of medicine: Eir (Norse)

goddess of nature: Isis (Egyptian)

goddess of power and destruction: Devi (Hindi)

goddess of spring: Maia (Greek)

goddess of stars: Sesheta (Egyptian)

goddess of the dawn: Chasca (Incan)

goddess of the forces of nature: Damia (Greek)

goddess of the harvest: Ceres (Roman)

goddess of the hearth: Hestia (Greek)

goddess of the hunt: Diana, Diane (Latin)

goddess of the moon: Deva (Hindi)

goddess of the sea: Sedna (Eskimo)

goddess of vengeance: Ara (Greek)

goddess of wine: Madira (Sanskrit)

goddess of wisdom: Athena (Greek)

goddess who gave birth to Diana and Apollo: Latonia (Latin)

God's gracious gift: Jania (Hebrew)

God's daughter: Basia (Hebrew)

God's decoration: Edian (Hebrew)

God's famous one: Tecia (Greek)

God's fire: Udiya (Hebrew)

God's garden: Karmel (Hebrew)

God's gift: Isoka (Nigerian)

God's gracious princess: Shantia (Greek)

Gods gracious woman: Rhian (Welsh)

God's happiness: Roniya (Hebrew)

God's light: Nuria (Aramaic), Uri (Hebrew)

God's name is divine: Theola (Greek)

God's precious butterfly: Janessa (Hebrew)

God's promise: Bessie, Betsy, Elisa, Elsa, Elsie, Helsa, Isa, Leeza, Olisa (Hebrew)

God's servant: Gilda (Celtic)

God's will: Uchenna (African)

gold: Golda (English), Iora (Latin), Koula (Tongan), Pazia (Hebrew), Zarina (Hindi), Zorina (Slavic)

golden: Aurel, Aurelia, Oralia, Oriel, Oriole, Orlena (Latin)

golden: Dior, Dore, Doreen (French)

golden: Ofira (Hebrew), Orla (Irish), Valora (Cambodian), Vanetta (Greek), Zarina (Hindi)

golden apple: Melora (Greek)

golden beauty: Orabel (French)

golden daughter: Chryseis (Latin)

golden dawn: Oriana (Latin)

golden flower: Chrissanth (French), Chrysanthe (Greek)

golden girl: Dorena (French)

golden haired: Pazia (Hebrew)

golden light: Ora (Hebrew)

golden prayer: Ora (Latin)

good: Agatha, Githa (Greek), Glenda (Welsh), Guda (Scandinavian), Hao (Vietnamese), Hasina (Swahili), Sai (Tongan), Sunee (Thai), Tovah, Yatva (Hebrew), Bona (Latin), Bonne, Bonnie (Scottish), Gasha (Russian)

good day: Bathanny (Aboriginal)

good fate: Fortuna, Fortune (Latin),

good fortune: Zaida (Arabic)

good lance: Rhonda (Welsh)

good looking: Farrah (English)

good news: Evangelina (Greek)

good reputation: Effie (Scottish)

good victory: Eunice (Greek)

goodness gracious: Lashanda (Hebrew), Lashawna, Lashonda (Irish)

goose: Chenetta (Greek)

grace: Ani (Polish) Kalasia, Kelesi (Tongan),

graced with God's bounty: Annelise, Grace, Gracia, Lariana, Torianna, Tristanne, Tyanna, Vienna (Latin)

graceful: Anais, Aniela, Anika, Anita, Annina, Anya, Chaanach, Chanina, Gratiana, Quiana, Veanna (Hebrew), Anja, Vanka, Vanya (Russian), Annabella, Annabelle (French), Anneka

(Dutch), Annelise (German), Annisa, Charis, Charissa, Charisse, Karis (Greek), Corolann, Diana, Diane, Jiana, Loriann, Nancy, Teanna (English), Engracia (Spanish), Linette (Celtic), Ona (Lithuanian), Vanni (Italian)

graceful dancer: Tautiti (Polynesian)

graceful Earth: Gaetana (Hebrew)

graceful farmer: Georgeanne (Greek), Georgianna (Latin)

graceful gazelle: Tabitha (Aramaic)

graceful great one: Titania (Greek)

graceful lily: Susan, Susannah (Hebrew)

graceful oak: Sheyenne (French)

graceful oak tree: Cheyenne (French)

graceful olive: Livana (Latin)

graceful one from Java: Javana (Malaysian)

graceful princess: Salliann (English), Tiana (Hebrew)

graceful rose: Roannah (Hebrew), Rosanna (English)

graceful siren: Loriann (English)

graceful third born child: Triana (Latin)

graceful victory: Brianna, Brianne (Celtic),

graceful violet flower: Vianna, Vianne (French)

graceful warrior: Luana (Hebrew)

gracious: Deanna (Latin), Winola (German)

gracious green springtime: Verdiana (Latin)

gracious queen: Royanna (English)

gracious victory: Breana (Celtic)

grand life: Roneisha (Welsh)

grandchild or the chief: Tierney (Irish)

grandfather: Poppy (English)

grandmother: Edda (Norse), Kui (Tongan)

grapes: Vinia (Latin)

grateful: Reiko (Japanese), Shakira (Arabic)

great: Dai (Japanese), Daron, Moreen (Irish), Indira (Hindi), Jalila (Arabic), Maja, Majid, Majid (Greek), Maybell (Latin), Moira (Gaelic), Nui (Maori), Viliya (Slavic)

great fair hair: Morgwen (Welsh)

great forest: Arden (Latin)

great glory: Vehka (Bulgarian)

great granddaughter: Nina, Ninetta (Spanish), Ninette (French)

great lord: Mahesa (Hindi)

great queen: Rhian (Welsh), Rianna (Irish)

great ruler: Meredith (Welsh)

great size and power: Titia (Greek)

great wisdom: Velika (Slavic)

greatest: Maxine (Latin)

greatest champion: Kenda, Kendra, Lakendra (Welsh)

greatly loved: Adorlee (Greek), Amada (Spanish), Amice, Amy (Latin)

Greek goddess: Shanda (Sanskrit)

green: Chloris, Phyllis (Greek), Midori (Japanese), Vrida (Spanish)

green gem: Cheryl (Welsh)

green gemstone: Emerald (French), Jade (Spanish)

green jewel: Beryl (Greek)

green like springtime: Verdi (Latin)

green shoot: Chloe (Greek)

green stone powering: Tiki, (Maori)

green-yellow: Chloris (Greek)

guarded: Samar, Samara, Samariah (Arabic), Selima (Scandinavian)

guarded by Ing: Inge (Norse), Atalaya (Spanish), Bakana (Aboriginal), Garda, Warda (German), Vedette (French)

guardian of the treasure: Gasparde (French)

guest: Sena, Xena, Zena (Greek)

guide from the forest: Guilda (Italian)

gypsy: Gitana (Spanish), Zigana (Hungarian)

H

half: Demi (French)

half Danish: Haldana (Norse)

halo : Hala (Arabic)

handsome: Alana, Alannah, Shakti (Hawaiian), Keverne (Gaelic), Alisa, Aliza, Yovela (Hebrew)

happiness: Gwyneth (Welsh), Leda (Greek), Leticia, Letisha, Letitia (Latin), Letty (English), Samina, Sananda, Syona (Hindi),

happy: Alaina, Mavia (Celtic), Alana, Alannah, Hoolana, Olina, Shakti (Hawaiian), Beata, Jonita, Laetitia, Lajoia, Latisha, Lecia, Leta, Shalita, Taesha (Latin), Cheera, Eunice, Lais, Lara, Larissa, Macria, Marcaria (Greek), Eda, Edith, Ida, Idabelle, Merinda, Summer, Sunny, Tate, Tish, Tisha (English), Felise, Joia, Lece (French), Saidah (Arabic), Sanyu (Native American), Kallolee (Hindi), Marney, Marnina (Israeli), Nara (Irish), Oseye (African), Rani, Rania, Roni, Ronli, Salida, Sasona, Tifara (Hebrew)

happy one from the green town: Phylicia (Latin)

happy pool: Merilyn (English)

happy time: Thana (Arabic)

hard working: Emere (Maori), Malika (Hungarian), Taleisha (Norse), Ida, Idabelle (English), Emily, Emma, Amelia, Ima, Ima, Induna, Milia, Milka, Milly, Shanida, Yamelia (German)

hard working warrior: Emmylou (German)

harmonious: Alina (Celtic), Harmony (Latin)

harmony: Alana, Alannah (Hawaiian), Amity (Latin)

harvest: Messina (Latin)

harvester: Reza (Slavic), Riza, Shantesa, Teresa, Teri, Terry, Theresa, Therese, Tess (Greek), Shanteca, Teca (Hungarian), Zilya (Russian)

has dark hair: Darcelle (French)

has supernatural powers: Eepa (Hawaiian)

hay meadow: Hailey, Haley, Hayley (English)

hazel nut: Aveline (German)

hazelnut tree: Hazel (English)

he has favored me: Ioana (Hebrew)

he sees: Jessica, Jessie (Hebrew)

headland: Nessa (Norse)

healer: Asa (Hebrew)

healing: Althea, Althea (Greek)

health: Elivira (Spanish), Siany (Irish)

healthy: Althea (Greek), Heloise (French), Lera (Russian), Marini (Swahili), Valentina, Valentine, Valerie (Latin), Wasila (English)

healthy wisdom: Sage (Latin)

hearing: Jimena (Spanish)

heart: Cordelia (Latin), Huette (German)

heather: Briar (French)

heaven: Jennalyn (Arabic), Kilia, Lani, Okilani (Hawaiian), Mapiya (Native American), Sema (Tongan), Urianna (Greek),

heavenly: Celena, Celeste, Celie, Celine, Olympia, Selena, Selene, Selina (Greek), Divinia (Latin), Divya (Hindi), Heavenly, Sky (English), Kimiko (Japanese)

heavenly branch: Laulani (Hawaiian)

heavenly caress: Mililiani (Hawaiian)

heavenly cloud: Aolani (Hawaiian)

heavenly flower: Pualani (Hawaiian)

heavenly inspiration: Ululani (Hawaiian)

heavenly rain: Ualani (Hawaiian)

heavenly rose: Roselani (Filipino)

heavenly shrine: Ahulani (Hawaiian)

heavy rain: Lovai (Tongan)

helmet: Billie, Elma, Elmina (German)

help: Bjorg (Scandinavian), Ophelia (Greek)

helped by God: Azelia (Hebrew)

helper: Alesia (Greek), Ozera (Hebrew), Tokoni (Tongan),

helper of humankind: Drina (Spanish)

helper to the priest: Camelia, Cami (Latin),

helpful: Aida (Latin), Ezra (Hebrew), Kodi (Irish)

her father rejoiced: Abbey (Hebrew)

her name is God: Sam, Samala, Samuela, Gabriella, Gabrielle, Gaby (Hebrew)

hero: Hailey (Scottish)

hero ruler of the battle: Valda (Norse)

heroine: Haley (Scandinavian)

heroine of God: Brielle (Hebrew)

hidden: Calypso (Greek)

hidden nook: Darnelle (English)

high: Alta (Latin), Bria (Gaelic), Vanna (English)

high clearing: Hayley (English)

high commander: Oma (Arabic)

high ranking: Armine, Irma (Latin)

highest order of the angels: Seraphina (Hebrew)

highest point of having: Lulani (Maori)

highest point of heaven: Lali (Spanish)

highly praised: Malina, Romia (Hebrew)

highly spirited: Jolie (English)

hill: Bria, Tannis (Gaelic), Brianna, Brianne (Celtic), Bryn (Welsh), Byanna (Irish), Geva (Hebrew), Olono (Aboriginal)

holly garden: Leslie (Gaelic)

holly tree: Hollis, Holly (English)

holy: Agnes, Ariadna, Ariadne, Loricia (Greek), Ariana, Lari, Lariana (Latin), Elga, Veta (Slavic), Glennis, Glynnis (Welsh), Helga (Norse), Liz, Lizabeth, Lizina (English), Lusa (Finnish), Olga (Scandinavian), Olienka (Russian), Santana (Spanish)

holy and sacred to God: Elise (French), Eliza, Elizabeth, Lyzabeth (Hebrew), Elka (Polish), Lisa (Greek), Yelisabeta (Russian)

holy crown of laurel leaves: Laricia (Latin)

holy God: Liesl (German)

holy to God: Libby, Marlis (Hebrew), Liese (German)

home: Dorma (Russian), Talena (Hebrew)

home in the valley field: Taya (Japanese)

home lover: Odette (French)

home ruler: Harriet (German)

honest: Honesta (Latin), Lalita (Sanskrit), Norleen (Irish), Onesta (English), Temina (Arabic), Thamah (Hebrew)

honestly: Noni (English)

honesty: Onora (English)

honey: Honey (English), Kameli (Hawaiian), Melina (Greek), Yaara (Hebrew)

honey wine: Meade (Greek)

honeybee: Lisa, Lissa, Melecent, Melissa, Melita (Greek), Missy (English), Shalisa (Hebrew)

honeysuckle tree: Lakkari (Aboriginal)

honey-sweet: Melita (Greek)

honor: Annora (Latin), Fola (African), Lamora (French),

honorable: Acacia (Spanish), Aneira (Welsh), Bria, Brianna, Brianne, Byanna (Celtic)

honorable: Brina, Ohnicio (Irish), Honor (Latin), Vandani (Hindi)

honored above all others: Sebastiana (Greek)

honor confers a crown: Sada (African)

honored: Efrata (Hebrew)

hope: Ashia (Arabic), Esperance (French), Hope (English), Nada, Nadia, Nadine (Russian), Santavana (Hindi), Zina, Carna, Nelia, Nell, Nellie (Latin), Karniela (Hebrew)

horn colored: Cornelia, Nelia (Latin)

horse goddess: Epona (Roman)

horse lover: Philippa (Greek)

horse rider: Tasida (Native American)

hospitable: Chimene (French), Sena, Xenia (Greek), Yachne (Hebrew)

hostage: Giselle (German)

hot: Chanda (Sanskrit)

house leader: Haliaka (Hawaiian)

house of God: Bethel (Hebrew)

hunter: Hunter (English), Winda (Swahili)

hunting rabbits: Heta (North American)

hyacinth: Iolanda (French), Jacinta, Jakinda (Spanish), Jolanda (Greek)

I

I love: Jaime, Jaimee (French)

ice: Crystal, Krystal (Greek)

idea: Pansy (French)

idle: Lundy (Welsh)

idol: Lanet, Lynette (Welsh)

idolized: Idola (Greek)

illusion: Maya (Hindi)

I'm on my way: Shania (Native American)

image: Imogene (Latin)

image of her mother: Imogene (Irish)

immortal: Ambrosia, Athanasia (Greek), Wahalla (Norse)

immortal wisdom: Phelia (Greek)

in bloom: Florence (Latin)

incense: Levona (Hebrew)

increasing: Olabasi (Nigerian)

independent: Neheda (Arabic)

Indian territory: Indiana (English)

indigenous: Haley (English)

indigo: Nili (Hebrew)

industrious: Alba (English), Amalea, Amaline, Amelia, Milly (German)

inheritance: Jerusha, Morasha (Hebrew)

inheritor: Ula (German)

inlet of water: Fleta (English)

innocence: Inocencia (Spanish), Lily (Latin)

innocent: Ayanna (Hindi), Bara, Denae (Hebrew)

inspiration: Musetta, Musette (French),

intelligent: Akilah, Akili (Arabic), Huette (English), Kyna (Irish), Zakia (Swahili)

intriguing: Zina (Irish)

invincible: Randi (English)

Ireland: Isla (Celtic)

iris flower: Iris (English)

island: Ila (French), Isola (Italian)

Italian town: Marsala (Italian)

ivory: Ivory (English)

ivory skin: Fiona (Gaelic)

ivy vine: Ivy (English)

J

jasmine flower: Jasmina, Jasmine, Jassi (Persian), Jessamine (French), Mali (Thai), Yasmine (Arabic),

jay bird: Jae (Latin)

jet stone: Siete (Tongan)

jewel: Amber (Arabic), Enya (Scottish), Gemma (Latin), Joyita (Spanish), Lakenya (African)

jewel crown: Tiara (Latin)

jewel flower: Tiulpe (Tongan)

jewel from the sea: Cordelia (Celtic)

jewel of the sea: Ujana (Celtic)

joining: Livia (Hebrew)

joy: Aine (Irish), Alisa, Aliza, Diza, Gila, Gilana (Hebrew), Ananda (Sanskrit), Bliss, Letty (English), Chara (Greek), Frayda (German), Joia (French), Latia (Latin), Maeve (Celtic)

joyful: Faina, Faine (English), Jocelyn, Jovi, Joy (Latin), Joyce (French)

joyful grace: Joyanna (English)

joyful part of a christmas song: Carolina (English)

joyful song: Rena (Hebrew)

juniper tree: Geneva (French)

just: Jocelyn (English)

justified: Dinah (Hebrew)

K

kernel: Eithne (Irish), Enya (Gaelic)

kind: Agatha (Greek), Edeline (German), Gasha (Russian), Lilo (Hawaiian)

kind young woman: Alma (Arabic)

kindhearted: Caron (Welsh), Ruta (Hebrew)

king: Ryann (Irish)

kingfisher bird: Sikota (Tongan)

kitten: Chita (Arabic), Kisa (Russian), Pala, Sanura (Swahili)

knowing right from wrong: Sanjana (Sanskrit)

knowledge: Bina (Hebrew), Kendra (English), Scienta (Latin)

knowledge seeker: Taliba (Arabic)

knowledgeable: Kenna (English)

L

lace: Leise (Polynesian)

lady: Domina (Latin), Donna, Ladonna (Italian), Kira (Russian)

lady: Leda (Greek), Marita, Martha (Aramaic), Nerys (Welsh)

lady from Cyprus: Cipriana (Italian)

lady from Rome: Romola (Latin)

lady of mercies: Mercedees (Spanish)

lady of sorrow: Marta (English)

lady of the house: Bibi (Persian)

lady of Zorro: Maita (Aramaic)

lady with the iron will: Isa (German)

lake: Ekala, Kolora, Nanda (Aboriginal), Inari (Finnish)

lamb: Cosette (German), Oona, Una (Irish), Rachelle, Raquel, Rachel (French)

lame: Claudia (French), Gladys (Latin)

land: Nuna (Native American), Terra (Latin)

large black bird: Raven (English)

large seabird: Sula (Icelandic)

large village house: Treveen (Welsh)

lark bird: Calandra (Greek)

late Summer: Reyhan, Teresa, Teri, Terry, Theresa, Therese, Tess, Toyah, Tracey, Tracie (Greek)

laughing: Kakata (Tongan), Kinta (Aboriginal), Rihsa (Latin),

laughter: Meara (Gaelic)

laurel: Loret, Loretta (Latin)

laurel leaves: Laura, Laurel, Lauren (Latin)

laurel tree: Daphne (Greek)

lava: Leura (Aboriginal)

lavender scent: Lavenita (Tongan)

lavender shrub: Laveni (Tongan)

law: Leya (Spanish), Nori (Japanese)

lay-abbot: Abbey (Scottish)

leader: Aubery (French), Llawella (Welsh)

leaf: Lou (Tongan)

leafy branch: Phyllis (Greek)

leaping running water: Tallulah (Native American)

leaping water: Tsula (Native American)

legal: Leanna, Leanne (French)

legendary bird: Jarita (Hindi)

lemon: Lamani (Tongan)

leopard: Lepati (Tongan)

level headed: Druella (Latin)

life: Aisha, Asha, Ashanti, Eshe, Iesha, Jakeisha, Lakeisha, Laneisha, Lekasha, Leneisha, Liesha, Nakeisha, Nekeisha, Quaneisha, Shaleisha, Taleisha (Swahili), Ashia, Hayat (Arabic), Ayasha (Persian), Betha (Celtic), Bethia (Gaelic), Chai, Chava, Chaya, Eva, Evaline, Eve, Haya, Ilisha, Neve (Hebrew), Evita (Spanish), Lide (Latin), Naeva (French), Niesha (African-American), Ola (Nigerian), Vica (Hungarian), Zoe (Greek), Zoia (Russian), Zoya (Slavic)

life meadow: Chaylea (English)

light: Aleena, Eleanor, Fotini, Layna, Leanore, Nora (Greek), Alina, Alina (Slavic), Amber (Egyptian), Ciana, Lina (Italian), Eli, Oleatha (Scandinavian), Ila (Hungarian), Ilene (Irish), Jyoti (Hindi), Laine, Lainey (English), Lucy, Takira (Latin), Liora,

Meira, Orah, Oralee, Orli, Yeira, Zehara (Hebrew), Malana, Shakti (Hawaiian), Meera (Israeli), Narelle (Aboriginal), Nura, Shera (Aramaic), Olena (Russian)

light and airy: Lana, Lanni (Hawaiian)

light fabric: Chambrray (French)

light hearted: Ulani (Hawaiian)

light of God: Eliora (Greek)

light olive color: Orna (Irish)

light purple color: Laveni (Tongan)

light purple colored flower: Lilac (English)

light skin: Orinda (Irish)

lightning: Levina (English), Uhila (Tongan)

like: Karalana (Greek), Kerenza (Hebrew)

like a lioness: Leandra, Leotina (Latin), Lenia (German)

like a song: Cantrelle (French)

like her mother: Vreneli (German)

like honey: Mel (Portuguese)

likeness: Imogene (Latin)

likeness to God: Meka, Micah, Mykaela, Shameka, Tashelle (Hebrew), Michelle, Nichelle (French)

Lila: Laikana (Tonga)

lilac flower: Lilac (English)

lily: Lile (Tongan), Lilia, Sukey (Hawaiian), Lilith, Lillian, Lilo (Latin), Lis (French), Sadira (Persian), Xuxa (Brazilian), Zosa (Swiss), Zusa (Slavic), Sana, Shana, Shanae, Sonel, Sue, Susie (Hebrew)

lily blossom: Yelena (Latin)

lily flower: Lilibeth (English), Lily (Latin), Sanne (Hebrew)

lily of the shining light: Sue-Ellen (Scottish)

lime: Laime (Tongan)

Lincoln's marsh: Lindsay (English)

linden tree: Lindy (English), Unnea (Norse)

linen: Llian (Welsh)

lion: Laione (Tongan)

lioness: Lea, Leah, Leigh, Leanna, Leanne, Leola, Liona, Loni, Shalona (Latin), Leolina, Llawella (Welsh), Leona (French)

lioness like: Leonie (French)

lioness of God: Ariel, Ariella, Lariel, Levia (Hebrew)

listener: Orell (Latin)

listening: Sam, Samariah, Simone, Tomone (Hebrew), Solada (Thai)

little: Bonita (Spanish), Etta (German), Isa (Greek), Linette (Celtic), Mina, Tahira, Timothea (English), Odelia (Scandinavian)

little armed warrior: Armida (Latin)

little ashes: Sindy (Greek)

little bagpipe: Musetta, Musette (French)

little bear: Ursa (Greek)

little Christian: Christie, Christina, Shantina (Latin), Christine (French)

little courageous woman: Carrie, Charlotte (French)

little crown of laurel leaves: Lorrelle (French)

little darling: Carina (Spanish), Darlilyn (English), Deleena (French)

little deer: Feena (Irish)

little determined guardian: Minka (Polish)

little dove: Calumina (Scottish), Yemina (Hebrew)

little elf: Elvina, Eriline (English)

little fairy: Pixie (English)

little fame: Cleo (Greek)

217

little farmer: Georgette (French)

little fiery one: Edana (Irish)

little flower: Pansy (Greek)

little gem: Jemma (English)

little gift: Doretta (Greek), Chavi (Gypsy), Chiquita, Nina, Ninetta (Spanish)

little girl: Lassie (Gaelic), Ninette (French), Shiquita (Spanish)

little graceful one: Lanet (Celtic), Nanetta, Nanette (French)

little lamb: Talya (Hebrew)

little lily: Suzette (French)

little lioness: Lionetta (Latin)

little love: Amorette (French), Amrita (Spanish)

little loved one: Luvena (Latin)

little miss: Missy (English)

little moon: Lunetta (Latin)

little mother: Umayma (Arabic)

little noble one: Patsy, Patrice, Patricia (Latin)

little noblewoman: Dama, Damita (Spanish)

little one: Latika (French), Totti (English)

little one with strength of God: Gable (French)

little pale one: Wannetta (English)

little pearl: Meg (Greek)

little priceless one: Netta (Latin)

little princess: Salette (English), Sarotte (French), Serita (Hebrew), Katina (Greek)

little raven: Brieena (Gaelic)

little rock: Roesia (German)

little rose: Charo, Zita (Spanish), Rosalind, Rosalind (Irish), Rosetta (Latin)

little saint: Santina (Spanish)

little Sally: Salette (English)

little Sam: Samia, Samia (Hebrew)

little sea friend: Irvette (English)

little she-bear: Ursula (Latin), Orsa (Greek), Orseline (Dutch)

little song lyric: Odelette (French)

little steady one: Pierette (French)

little stone: Perette (French)

little stranger: Babette (Greek)

little strong and courageous woman: Lotte, Sharlote (French), Letty (English)

little swallow: Celandine (Greek)

little thing: Cosette (French)

little truthful one: Ally (Greek)

little victory: Lorrelle (French)

little victory of the people: Nicoletta, Nicollete (French)

little warrior: Bernadette, Bernadine (French),

little weak one: Claudette (French)

little wished for: Manette (Latin), Manka (Polish), Manon (French),

little woman: Carlotta, Carolina (Italian)

little youth: Juliet (French)

little youthful one: Lajuliette (Latin)

lively: Bibiana (Latin), Gai, Gay (French), Gaylia (English)

lively singer: Gail (English)

lives in the valley: Deana, Deanna (English)

living: Chava (Hebrew)

lofty: Aaliyah (Arabic), Elata (Latin)

logical: Ilysa (Greek)

long-lived: Amarinda (Greek), Hisa (Japanese)

look out: Bakana, Narlala (Aboriginal)

lord: Cirilla, Cyra (Greek), Dominica, Domino (Latin), Kami (Japanese)

lordly: Kyrene (Greek)

lordly ruler: Cyria, Cyrilla (Greek)

lost love: Lorna (English)

lotus flower: Kamala (Sanskrit), Lien (Chinese), Lotus (Greek)

loud: Tristen (Latin)

loud thunder: Taima (Native American)

lovable: Amabel, Amanda, Ambel (Latin), Annabella, Annabelle (French)

love: Asta (Greek), Carey, Cari (Gaelic), Carita, Jovanna (Latin), Carys, Cerys (Welsh), Hawa (Arabic), Kama (Sanskrit), Kerensa (English), Lalasa (Hindi), Larmina (German), Mahal (Filipino), Mina (German), Aasta (Nordic)

love me: Femi (Nigerian)

loved: Deveney (Scottish), Eme, Mirena (Hawaiian), Lovisa (English), Priya (Latin), Sheri (French)

loved aunt: Ammu (Arabic)

loved by the people: Lida, Ludmilla, Mila (Slavic)

loved friend: Amice (Latin)

loved memory: Mina (German)

lovely: Hermosa (Latin), Jamila (Arabic), Nava, Navit (Hebrew), Yoshe (Japanese), Zurafa (Arabic)

lovely one: Calandra (Greek)

lover: Induna (Norse)

lover of flowers: Philantha (Greek)

lover of horses: Pippa (Greek)

lover of humankind: Philana (Greek)

lover of songs: Philomela (Greek)

loving: Caron (Welsh), Chahna (Hindi), Karenza (English), Pam (Greek)

loyal: Leala (French), Leandra (Latin), Vera (Russian)

loyalty: Leya (Spanish)

luck: Clover (English)

lucky: Faustine (Latin), Felise (French), Fortuna, Fortune (Italian), Ganesa (Hindi), Halona (Native American), Monifa (African), Otilie (Slavic), Sadiya, Saidah, Zada (Arabic)

lucky star: Mazal (Hebrew)

luna: Solita (Hindi)

lyre music: Lirit (Greek)

M

magic power: Wakanda (Native American)

magical being: Alvina, Elvina (English), Aubery (French)

magnolia tree blossom: Magnolia (Latin)

magpie: Kirra (Aboriginal)

maiden: Cora, Coralee, Corinne (Greek), Ginia (Latin), Imogene (Irish), Mada, Maddie, Madeleine, Madge (Hebrew)

maize: Maisie (French)

majestic: Alta, Alta (Latin), Basillia (Greek)

make famous: Tani (Spanish)

maker of music: Hula (Hebrew)

mallow flower: Malva, Melba (Latin)

manly: Andra, Andria, Andriana (Greek), Polly (Hebrew)

marjoram: Marjolaine (French)

mark by burning: Brenda (English)

marriage: Jerusha (Hebrew)

marsh: Lundy (Gaelic)

marsh flower: Marice (German)

marshland: Brie (French)

meadow: Lea, Leah, Leigh (English)

measure: Tannis (Arabic)

medicine woman: Yenene (Native American)

meeting: Losaki (Polynesian)

melody: Aria, Arietta (Italian), Mangena, Marah (Hebrew),

Odele (French), Taraneh (Persian)

melon: Meleni (Tongan)

Mel's friend from the mill: Melva, Melvina (Gaelic), Merva (Irish)

merchant: Yamilla (Slavic)

merciful: Clementia, Clementine, Osanna (Latin), Hanele (Hebrew), Mileta (German), Myla (English)

mercy: Mercia, Mercy (English)

mermaid: Miranda (Latin), Morina (Irish)

messenger: Aharona (Arabic), Cami, Camilla (French), Herma (Greek)

messenger of God: Angel, Angelina, Angeline, Aniela, Engel, Engelina, Evangelina (Greek), Arella (Hebrew)

middle child: Meda, Meda, Messina (Latin)

mighty: Rayna (Scandinavian)

mighty grace: Reanna (German)

mighty in battle: Matilda (German)

mighty warrior ruler: Jerica (German)

mild: Milena (German)

Milky Way galaxy: Kaniva (Tongan)

miller: Mileta (Latin)

mind: Huette (German)

mine: Keli (Tongan), Mia (Italian)

mint: Miniti (Tongan)

miracle: Mana (Tongan)

miracle child: Mirica (Latin)

miracle of God: Nasya (Hebrew)

mirror: Kyoko (Japanese)

mirror reflection: Toshi (Japanese)

moderation: Temperance (Latin)

modest: Haidee (Greek), Haya (Arabic), Modesty (Latin),

moody: Doreen (Irish)

moon: Alina, Jannali, Keina (Aboriginal), Chandra, Chandria, Lachandra (Sanskrit), Celena, Celeste, Celie, Celine, Cynthia, Selena, Selene, Selina, Solina (Greek), Kamaria (African), Lewanna (Hebrew), Lucine (Arabic), Luna (Latin), Sale (Hindi)

moon goddess: Artemis (Greek)

moonlight: Chandani (Hindi), Mahina (Hawaiian)

morning: Saba (Arabic), Zephira (Hebrew)

morning dew drops: Talor (Hebrew)

morning east wind: Sabiya (Arabic)

morning star: Danica (Slavic)

morning sun: Levania (Latin)

most beautiful: Alika (Nigerian), Calida (Spanish), Vassy (Persian), Clarest (French)

mother: Janaki (Hindi), Maia, Maja (Greek), Matrika (Sanskrit), Uma (Hindi)

mother of Aphrodite: Dione (Greek)

mother of the gods: Cybil (Greek)

motherly: Macawi (Native American)

mothers gift: Meena (Greek)

mound of earth: Zolah (Italian)

mountain: Radwa, Sidra (Arabic)

mountain climber: Parvati (Sanskrit)

mountain goat: Yael (Hebrew)

mountain lake: Tarne (Scandinavian)

mountain or strength: Arnina (Hebrew)

mountain that is small: Shaila (Hindi)

mountain top: Samya (Arabic)

much desired: Desire, Desiree (French)

much loved: Cara (Italian), Carina (Latin), Cherelle, Cherry (French), Chika (Japanese), Dodie (Hebrew), Taffy, Taffine (Welsh)

mulberry tree: Syke (Greek)

muse: Musetta, Musette (French)

mushroom: Bambra (Aboriginal)

music: Melody (Greek)

musical instrument: Ruana, Ruana (Hindi), Vinna (Italian)

my: Mimi (French)

my lady: Milada (English)

my love: Milada (Slavic)

my song: Shiri (Hebrew)

my song is happiness: Ronena (Hebrew)

myrrh: Myra (Latin)

myrtle tree: Hestia (Persian), Lilipilli (Aboriginal), Makala (Hawaiian)

N

nail: Clove (Latin)

named child: Jina (Swahili)

narrow: Kyle (Irish)

narrow lane or little road: Lane (English)

narrow valley between the hills: Glenna (Irish)

nation: Ululani (Hebrew)

nativity: Tashelle (Hebrew)

near and dear: Chika (Japanese)

near the graceful one: Byanna (English)

near to heaven: Pililani (Hawaiian)

neat: Delyth (Welsh)

necessity: Ananke (Greek)

necklace: Lavani (Tongan)

nest: Nidra (Latin)

new: Nova, Novella, Novia (Latin)

new moon: Micina, Migina (Native American), Mika (Japanese), Neoma (Greek), Tain (Hawaiian)

newcomer: Novella (Latin)

next: Nydia (Latin)

night: Koko (Native American), Ratri (Hindi)

night beauty: Layla, Leila (Arabic),

night time: Yamini (Hindi)

ninth: Noni (Latin)

ninth born child: Nona (Latin)

ninth child: Anona (Latin)

noble: Ada (Latin), Adina, Elicia (Hebrew), Akela, Aleka (Hawaiian), Adalia, Adela, Adelaide, Alarice, Alice, Alicia, Alison, Allison, Ally, Athela, Edeline, Elisha, Elka, Elke, Elli, Elsa, Elsie, Idelia, Ilise (German), Alba, Almira, Earlene, Elmina, Ethel (English), Ela (Polish), Heidi (Swiss), Karima (Arabic), Ellice, Euganie, Eugaenia, Gena, Ilysa (Greek), Elva, Elvie, Elvy, Moina, Mona (Irish), Irma, Imrina, Letricia, Nola, Nolana, Ormanda, Patty, Petica, Trisha (Latin), Licha (Spanish), Marquise (French), Sujata (Hindi), Yevgenia (Russian)

noble birth: Ada (Latin)

noble excellence: Ujana (African)

noble lady: Freya (Scandinavian)

noble protector: Delana, Delma (German)

noble strength: Audrey (English)

noble woman: Hermoine (Greek), Ilsa (German)

noisy: Shandy (English), Sona (Latin)

not jealous: Azelia (Greek)

O

oak: Eilah (Hebrew), Nara (Japanese)

oak tree: Alona (Latin), Chenetta (French), Elana (Hebrew), Ituha (Native American)

oak tree with a vine: Papina (Native American)

ocean: Kamoana (Hawaiian), Thalassa (Greek)

ocean waves: Leakiki (Polynesian)

of high degree: Arminda, Larnelle (Latin)

of Olympus: Olympia (Greek)

of the court: Courtney (English)

of the fatherland: Odette (German)

of the moon: Lekeleka (Tongan)

of the sea: Marina (Latin)

of the sea: Morgan (Celtic)

offering: Portia (Latin)

old: Alda (German), Saarah, Yeshisha (Hebrew), Shannon (Gaelic)

old friend: Olwyn (English)

old soul: Elli (Norse)

oleander: Oliana (Polynesian)

olive: Liv (Latin)

olive: Zeta (Hebrew)

olive colour: Ornice (Irish)

olive tree: Livia, Olive, Olivia (Latin)

one: Oona, Umniya (Latin)

one thousand: Osen (Japanese)

one who baptizes: Baptisa (Latin)

one who brings happiness: Ahyoka (Native American)

one who brings joy: Peata (Maori)

one who broods: Delilah (Hebrew)

one who chatters: Chiku (Swahili)

one who gives support: Saada (Hebrew)

one who has goals: Nyssa (Latin)

one who hears the voices of the forest: Seda (Armenian)

one who helps: Socorro (Spanish)

one who hesitates: Kali (Hawaiian)

one who hides: Calypso (Greek)

one who honors God: Timothea (Greek)

one who is admired: Vonda (Irish)

one who is always there: Killara (Aboriginal)

one who is expected: Oneida (Native American)

one who is forgiven: Kaiyo (Japanese)

one who is safe: Salma (Swahili)

one who is veiled: Filma (German)

one who listens: Sherika (Arabic)

one who lives by the ocean: Jalini (Hindi)

one who lives in the valley: Odelia (English)

one who plants: Tanita (Hebrew)

one who provokes: Savitri (Sanskrit)

one who shines: Mahla (Hebrew)

one who shines brightly from within: Berdine (German)

one who struggles: Hedda (German)

one who supplants: Jaime, Jaimee (Hebrew)

one who talks at night: Samar, Samara, Samariah (Arabic)

one who thinks of the sea: Halimeda, Hallie (Greek)

one who trembles: Raama (Hebrew)

one who understands: Samia (Arabic)

one who was honored: Taka (Japanese)

one who worships: Takia (Arabic)

one with compassion: Daya (Sanskrit)

one with the gap in her tooth: Masani (Swahili)

only child: Kamea (Hawaiian)

opal gem: Opeli (Tongan)

open field: Velda (German)

open grassland: Savanna (Latin)

orange: Moli (Tongan), Saffron (Arabic)

orange tree: Alani (Hawaiian)

orchard: Carma (Arabic), Carmen, Carmine (Hebrew), Oketa (Tongan)

orchid flower child: Orchio (Italian)

order: Cosima (Greek)

ornament of the Lord: Adiel (Hebrew)

owl: Lulu (Tongan)

owner of the new house: Xaveria (Spanish)

P

pale skinned: Wanda (English)

palm tree: Tama, Tamara, Tamesha, Thamar (Hebrew)

palm tree leaf: Sansana (Hebrew)

palm tree shoot: Batul (Arabic)

pansy flower: Panisi (Tongan)

parrot: Akala (Aboriginal)

passion flower: Kohia (Polynesian)

passionate: Chanda (Sanskrit)

passover: Pascale, Pascha (French)

pastures: Arva (Latin)

pathway: Keala (Hawaiian)

patient: Patience (Latin)

pawpaw: Lesi (Tongan)

peace: Chezna (Slovak), Erin, Erinna (Irish), Hopi (North American), Ira, Reena, Rene (Greek), Selam (Ethiopian), Jonita, Selima, Shaanana, Shalva, Zulema (Hebrew), Malina (Hawaiian), Tula (Hindi), Ululani (Sanskrit), Serena, Serene, Serenity (Latin)

peace is announced: Kasimira (Slavic)

peace is proclaimed: Kazimiera (Polish)

peaceful: Ahuda (Hebrew), Alana, Alannah (Hawaiian), Eirene, Evania, Irene (Greek), Freda, Freida, Gabriella (German), Jereni, Orina, Orya (Russian), Salama (Arabic), Tullia (Irish), Winnie (English), Yani (Aboriginal)

peaceful dove: Colina (Irish)

peaceful healer: Eir (Norse)

peaceful home: Emmaline (French)

peaceful ruler: Farica, Frederica, Frederique, Ricki (German)

peaceful silence: Tacey (English)

peacefulness: Malu (Hawaiian)

peacemaker: Farica (German), Mereki (Aboriginal)

peach tree: Peaches (English)

pear: Rissa (Greek)

pear tree: Perry (French)

pearl: Chu (Chinese), Ghita, Perlita (Italian), Gita, Markita (Slavic), Greta, Gretel, Maggie, Maretta, Margie, Margaret, Margo, Meagan, Megan, Peggy (Greek), Gretchen (German), Lulu (Arabic), Marguerite (French), Maria, Marie (Hebrew), Marjorie (Scottish) Pearl (English)

pecking bird: Luyu (Native American)

pelican: Shada (Native American)

penny coin: Peneli, Penelope, Penny (Greek)

people: Tami (Japanese)

people of God: Elama (Greek)

people of victory: Colette (French)

perfect: Dilys (Welsh)

perfection: Kamilah, Kamille (Arabic), Krita (Sanskrit), Tamara, Tamesha (Hebrew),

perfume: Kaloni (Tongan), Kaoru (Japanese)

perhaps: Malia, Maliaka (Hawaiian)

picked flower: Mansi, Mausi (Native American)

picture: Omemee (Native American)

pigeon: Kereru, Polynesian, Tama (Hebrew)

pine nuts burning: Kulya (Native American)

pine tree: Orinda (Hebrew)

pine tree child: Matsuko (Japanese)

pineapple: Anona (Latin)

pink or white blossom: May (Latin)

pious: Pia (Italian)

pipe: Chanel (French)

pipe layer: Piper (English)

place of dust: Ophra, Oprah (Hebrew),

place of pleasure: Eden (Hebrew)

place of possums: Marree (Aboriginal)

place of rest: Kaya (Japanese)

place where rushes grow: Kogarah (Aboriginal)

plain: Macha (Irish)

plant: Neta, Shaneta (Hebrew)

planter: Shanisa (Hebrew)

Platypus: Gayadin (Aboriginal)

player of the harp: Lyris (Greek)

playful: Jodi, Jodie, Jody (Latin), Lalita (Sanskrit),

pleasant: Effie (Greek), Farrah (English), Naomi, Navit (Hebrew)

pleasant companion: Anisah (Arabic)

pleasant life: Eveleen (Celtic)

pleasing: Deka (Somalian)

pleasure: Delicia (English)

pledge: Giselle (German)

plenty: Idelle (Celtic), Koora (Aboriginal), Myra (Greek),

plenty of grass seed: Merrina (Aboriginal)

poem: Mele (Hawaiian)

poet: Deveney (Irish)

poetry: Awena (Welsh), Edda (Norse), Poeta (Italian), Rima (Spanish)

polished: Mahla (Hebrew)

polished jewel: Talya (Japanese)

polisher: Buffy (English)

polite: Mirna, Myrna (Irish), Rei (Japanese)

pool of water: Piscina (Italian)

poppy flower: Polla (Arabic), Poppy (English), Rea (Greek)

possesses strength: Bedelia (French)

possessor of sacred wisdom: Verena, Verene (Swiss)

possum: Kara, Karalana (Aboriginal)

pour: Serah (Hebrew)

powerful: Adira (Hebrew), Arnelle, Anrette, Aubery (French), Edrea (English), Qadiri (Arabic), Raina (German), Rhonda (Welsh), Ronalda (Norse)

powerful army commander: Harriet (French)

powerful princess: Valeska (Polish)

powerful protector: Vallia (Spanish)

powerful warrior: Tilda (German)

prairie flower: Leotie (Native American)

prairie hen: Kewanee (Native American)

praise God: Athalia (Hebrew)

praise to God: Odelia (Hebrew)

praised: Elata (Latin), Jodi, Jodie, Jody, Judith, Judy (Hebrew), Samena (Arabic), Yudita (Russian)

praised by God : Acima (Hebrew)

praised highly: Marlene (Hebrew)

praising God: Tacita (Hebrew)

prayer: Mani, Chinese, Osanna, Preya (Latin), Yashna (Hindi)

prayerful: Arabella (Latin)

precious: Alani, Alanis (German), Chen (Chinese), Nadira (Arabic), Treasure (English), Yakira (Hebrew)

precious gemstones: Jewel (French)

precious jewel: Opal (Sanskrit)

precious or graceful gemstone: Jewelana (English)

precious treasure: Takara (Japanese)

pregnant: Cyma (Greek)

pretty: Bonita, Linda, Lindie, Lynda, Linda (Spanish), Bonne, Bonnie (Scottish), Jolena, Jolie (French), Keiko (Japanese), Lawan (Thai), Marini (Swahili)

pretty flower: Lomasi (North American)

pretty jay bird: Jalinda (Spanish)

pretty roses: Roseanne (English)

prevailing: Vincentia, Vincenza, Vincenzia (Latin)

priceless: Antoinette, Antonia (French), Toinette, Toni, Tonia (Greek), Tolla (Polish), Tonneli (Swiss), Taula (Tongan)

primrose flower: Primrose (English)

princess: Almira, Amira, Elmira, Saarah (Arabic), Earlene, Salena (English), Gladys (Celtic), Sade, Sadie, Sally, Sara, Saree, Sari, Sarice, Sarika, : Sarina, Sarinha, Sarita, Saronna, Shara, Sharae, Suri, Sydelle, Xara, Zahira, Zali (Hebrew), Sale (Hawaiian), Sasa (Hungarian), Sirri (Finnish), Soraya (Persian), Zaidee (Irish)

princess from the pool: Sharolyn (Hebrew)

princess from the rocky hill: Satara (Hebrew)

princess of Panchala: Panchali (Sanskrit)

prisoner: Bandi (Arabic)

probably: Malia, Maliaka (Hawaiian)

proclaimer: Clio (Greek)

projected: Hilma (German)

promise: Arlene (Gaelic), Eriline, Larlene (Celtic), Gisela, Jizelle (German), Horatia (Greek), Sheba (Hebrew)

promise by God: Amaris (Hebrew)

proper: Yaminah (Arabic)

property guardian: Eddi (English)

prophet: Cassie, Cassandra, Cybil, Krisandra, Sibyl, Sybil (Greek), Edris (Welsh), Sevilla (Spanish)

prosperous: Alda (German), Eadda, Edina, Edith, Edlyn, Ida, Idabelle, Shanice, Uda, Udele, Yudelle (English), Mieko (Japanese), Mira, Mirabel (Latin), Peri (Greek), Riddhi (Sanskrit)

prosperous one: Renny (Irish)

protected: Kiva (Hebrew)

protected by the Lord: Hasia (Hebrew)

protecting guardian: Villette (Russian)

protecting hands: Ramona (Spanish)

protection: Billie, Elma, Elmina, Helma, Vilhelmina, Vilhelmine, Wileen, Willa, Wilma (German), Larina, Larine (Latin),

protector: Aminta (Greek)

protector of human kind: Olesia (Polish)

protector with a sword: Giselle (English)

pure: Agnes, Caron, Phoebe (Greek), Bianca, Febe (Italian), Caitlin, Kaitlin (Irish), Candy, Lovinia (Latin)

pure light: Kayalana (Greek)

pure one from the meadow: Keighlea (Irish)

pure one whose God is gracious: Kooanna (Greek)

pure white: Candice, Dacia (Greek),

purity: Adara, Fadila, Safa, Safiya, Salihah, Tahira, Zaira

(Arabic), Caryn (Danish), Cathleen, Ina (Irish), Catrina (Slavic), Catherine, Cathy, Karan, Karen, Karida, Kassia, Kate, Kath, Katherine, Kathleen, Kay, Neysa, Parthena (Greek), Chastity, Ginia, Ginny, Laveda, Lavina, Lavinia, Lily, Virginia, Virtue (Latin), Conchetta (Italian), Inez, Inocencia (Spanish), Kaisa (Swedish), Kakalina (Hawaiian), Kanya (Hindi), Kateri (Native American), Katrina (Scandinavian), Kayla, Purity (English), Keja (Swedish), Nessa (Norse), Rayleen (Hebrew), Trina (Scandinavian), Zakiya (Swahili)

purple: Giacitna (Italian), Iolanda (French)

purple: Jacy, Jacinda, Jacinta, Jakinda (Spanish), Jolanda, Yola, Yolanda (Greek)

purple color: Maeve (Gaelic)

purple flower: Lantha (Greek)

purple gemstone: Amethyst (Greek)

push away with the foot: Hateya (Native American)

Q

queen: Darice, Zenanda (Persian), Kuini (Tongan), Lareina, Reina (Spanish), Malha, Sheba (Hebrew), Malka (Arabic), Raine, Regina (Latin), Rane, Rani (Scandinavian), Riona (Irish)

queen of the heavens: Hera (Greek), Juno (Latin)

quick: Miki (Hawaiian), Shakeena (Irish)

quiet: Shizu, Yoshi (Japanese)

R

radiance: Zara (Arabic)

rain: Amarina, Tallara (Aboriginal), Reva (Hebrew), Uha (Tongan), Varsha (Hindi)

rain falling: Huyana (Native American)

rainbow: Enfys (Welsh), Iris (Greek), Keshet (Hebrew)

raining: Dima (Hebrew)

raining at night: Amaya (Japanese)

rainy: Raina (English)

rare: Selda (English)

raven: Leveni (Tongan)

raven haired: Brieena (Gaelic)

ray of light: Huelo (Tongan), Keren (Hebrew), Kiran (Hindi)

reaffirming the belief in God: Ezrela (Hebrew)

rebel: Renita (Latin), Roula (Greek)

rebellious: Meri (Hebrew)

reborn: Renee (French), Shinae (Irish)

red: Akako (Japanese), Carmine (Latin), Omaira (Arabic)

red clouds in the sunset: Sanuye (Native American),

red color: Scarlett (English)

red earth: Adama (Latin)

red flowering tree: Waratah (Aboriginal)

red haired: Flanna, Flannery (Irish), Ginger (English), Rufina (Italian)

red or brown complexion: Cera (Irish) (Welsh)

red or yellow translucent gemstone: Carnelian (Latin)

red water lily: Nerida (Aboriginal)

reddish brown color: Sorrell (French)

reddish or brown hair: Fawn (French)

reflected sound: Echo (Greek)

reflection: Kagami (Japanese)

regal ruler: Alarice (German)

reliable: Ethana (Hebrew), Onesta (English)

religious service: Mela (Hindi)

religious teachings: Nori (Japanese)

remembrance: Deja (Spanish)

renewed strength: Reubena (Latin)

renewer: Eddi (Hebrew), Edna, Ena, Adara (Hebrew), Ludella (English)

renowned in the land: Rolanda (Latin)

renowned ruler: Valancia (German)

replacer: Jaci, Jacinda, Jacki, Jacky, Jacqui, Jacqueena, Jami, Jamie (Hebrew), Jacqueline (French)

replacer from the pool: Jamilynn (English)

replacer queen: Jacqueena (Hebrew)

resemblance: Halina (Greek)

resolute guardian: Wilona (German)

respectable: Efrata (Hebrew)

rest: Roesia (German)

rest of life: Hawa (Hebrew)

restful: Sabra (Arabic)

resurrection: Anastasia, Stacey, Stacia (Greek), Nitasse (French)

revelation of God: Tiffany (Greek)

reward: Aida (Arabic), Mercia, Mercy (Spanish)

rewards: Lucita (Latin)

rhyme: Rima (Spanish)

rhythm: Cadence (Latin)

rich: Ashira (Hebrew)

rich and powerful: Richelle (German)

rich powerful ruler: Ricki (German)

rich reward: Lakresha (Latin)

riches: Lucita (Latin)

rider of horses: Rechaba (Hebrew)

right: Yaminah (Arabic)

right star: Maia (Greek)

righteous: Justine (Latin)

righteous child: Kimiko (Japanese)

ripple: Taral (Hindi)

rising: Rukiya (Swahili), Samya (Hebrew)

rising or ascending: Aaliyah, Aleah, Aliya (Hebrew)

rising sun: Levana (Latin)

rival: Emily, Emma (Latin), Kalinn (Scandinavian), Lira (Aboriginal), Tyne (English), Varana (Hindi)

river bend: Nyah (Aboriginal)

robin bird: Lopini (Tongan), Robin (English)

rock: Callan (Scottish), Peita, Peta (Greek)

rocking motion: Vellamo (Finnish)

rocky hill: Latara (Irish)

Roman goddess: Annona (Greek)

Roman goddess of good fortune: Felicity (Latin)

Roman warrior: Romelda (German)

roots run deep: Nitara (Hindi)

rope: Nata (Hindi)

rosary: Charo (Latin), Rosaria, Rosario (Italian)

rose: Losa (Polynesian), Rasia, Rhodelia (Greek), Rhonwen (Celtic), Roesia (French), Raisa, Raizel, Shana, Shanae (Hebrew), Roisin (Irish), Rosa (Latin), Rosina (English), Rosita (Spanish), Roza, Ruza (Slavic), Varda, Vardina, Vardis (Arabic)

rose flower: Rose, Rosie (English),

Rosebud: Kalika (Greek)

rosemary herb: Rosemary (Latin)

rosy cheeked: Pippi (French), Rhodelia (Greek)

rough island: Rona (Norse)

round basket: Spira (Greek)

royal: Basillia (Greek), Imeria (Latin), Kim (English)

royal grace: Rayann (French)

royal messenger: Aulani (Hawaiian)

ruby: Ruby (French)

rule temptress: Raelene (Latin)

ruler: Arica, Erica (Scandinavian), Arika (Norse), Isolde (German), Medora (Greek), Norma (Hawaiian), Ricca (Spanish), Rika (Swedish), Rula (Latin)

ruler of the house: Enrica (Spanish), Henrietta (French), Yetta (English)

runaway: Sharda (Arabic)

runs away: Sharda (English)

S

Sabines: Sabina (Latin)

sacred: Elga (Slavic), Leeza, Libby, Marlis (Hebrew), Lehua (Hawaiian), Liese, Liesl (German)

sacred and holly to God: Lilibeth (English)

sacred bells: Kerani (Hindi)

sacred dancer: Kachine, Satinka (Native American)

sacred god: Liz, Liza, Liza (English)

sacred purity: Sanchia (Latin)

sacred river: Yamuna (Hindi)

sacred to God: Lizabeth, Lizina (English), Lusa (Finnish), Veta (Slavic)

sacred tree: Sala (Hindi)

sacrifice: Natara (Arabic)

sad: Trista (Latin)

safe: Salima (Arabic)

safe refuge: Nydia (Latin)

sailor: Ormanda (German)

saint: Muna (Basque), Richael (Irish), Sangata (Tongan), Santana, Shantana (Spanish)

saint worshipper: Nevina (Irish)

saintly: Riona (Irish), Shantaina (Spanish)

salt water: Tarni (Aboriginal)

salty: Hala (Latin)

salvation: Bjorg (Scandinavian)

sanctuary in battle: Avice (German), Avis (English)

sand piper: Pipipa (Aboriginal)

sandalwood: Rohana (Hindi)

sapphire: Safaia (Tongan), Sapphire, Sapphira (Greek)

satin: Satini (Tongan)

satisfaction: Revaya (Hebrew)

saved: Moesha (Hebrew), Moselle (French), Mosina (French)

saw: Prisma (Greek)

saw toothed: Sidra (Spanish)

Saxon: Sass (Irish)

scarlet: Carmine (Latin)

scented oil: Myra (Latin)

sea: Kai, Kailani (Hawaiian), Legana, Legana (Aboriginal), Maren (Latin), Marita (Spanish), Nyree (Maori), Thalassa (Greek)

sea bright: Muriel (Irish)

sea daughter: Dilija (Polish)

sea fairy: Nerine (Greek)

sea flower: Puakai (Hawaiian)

sea lord: Meredith (Welsh)

sea nymph: Nerida, Nerina (Greek)

sea of fire: Enakai (Hawaiian)

sea urchin: Vana (Polynesian)

sea woman: Pania (Maori)

seabird: Larana (Latin)

seafarer: Irva (English)

seagull: Tala (Tongan), Yara, Yarna (Aboriginal)

seal: Romola (Irish)

seashore: Arva (Latin)

season of harvest: Autumn (Latin)

seawater: Tahi (Tongan)

second born child: Ulu (African)

second born twin: Kakra (Ghanaian)

secret: Bian (Vietnamese), Samena (Tongan)

secure: Selima (Arabic)

seductive: Blanda (Latin)

see fairy: Rissa (Greek)

seed: Sada (English)

seeds: Rudra (Hindi), Zera (Latin)

seeds in the basket: Huata (North American)

seeker: Petula (Latin), Sheridan (Gaelic)

sees the bright side of a situation: Pollyana (English)

self-love: Narcisse (French)

semi-precious gem: Amber (Arabic)

sensible: Alyssa (Greek)

sensitive: Mana (Japanese)

sent from heaven: Okalani (Hawaiian)

seraph: Seraphina (Hebrew)

serene: Ela (Polish), Sarila, Sarina, Serena, Serene, Serenity (Latin)

serenity of the skies: Nalani (Hawaiian)

serpent: Lilith (Hebrew), Lindy (German)

seventh daughter: Bathsheba, Sheba, Yvonne (Hebrew)

shadow: Zillah (Hebrew)

sharp tempered: Asperity (English)

she: Elle (French)

she brings good news: Lia (Greek)

she cries: Aleela (Swahili)

she has a crown of laurel leaves: Lorielle (Latin)

she has a heart and soul: Janan (Arabic)

she honours God: Timi (English)

she is a little like a rock: Rochelle (French)

she is a rose: Rozelle (Greek)

she is a star: Estelle (French)

she is brave: Shakeena (Irish)

she is darling: Darnelle (Irish)

she is famous: Rudelle (French)

she is for me: Mili (Israeli)

she is freedom: Cella (Italian)

she is from the channel: Shanelle (French)

she is gracious to God: Jonelle (French)

she is grand: Ronelle (Welsh)

she is loved: Filomena, Philomena (Greek), Lovai (English), Sherelle, Katrinelle, Lavelle (French), Shakara (Danish)

she is singing: Rania (Hebrew)

she is the alluring one: Lorielle (French)

she is the harvester: Terelle (Greek)

she is the pretty one: Shakila (Arabic)

she is unity: Sheona (Irish)

she is victory: Lorrelle (English)

she looks like a loved relative: Halia (Hawaiian)

she oak tree: Lemana (Aboriginal)

she who is dark: Kerrielle (Celtic)

shell: Concha (Spanish)

shellfish: Kahi (Tongan)

shelter: Garda (Norse)

shield: Randi (English)

shield bearer: Thyra (Greek)

shining: Marmara, Marney, Marnina, Phoebe (Greek), Bertha, Sunshine (English), Febe (Italian)

shining light: Aileen, Ena (Irish), Alaina, Elli, Lene (German), Alena, Jelena, Lelya, Yalena, Yeira, Liolya, Yelenah (Russian), Annora, Eileen, Elena, Eleni, Elle, Helen, Helena, Lenore, Nitsa, Ronaele (Greek), Ellen (Scottish), Ilona, Lenci, Onella (Hungarian), Lena, Leni (Latin), Lenora (Italian), Leora, Zizi (Hebrew), Roshan (Sanskrit) ,

shining like a star: Sidba (Latin)

shining moon: Launoa (Tongan)

shining sea: Meryl (Irish)

shining upon man: Cassie, Cassandra, Kassandra (Greek)

shiny: Satin (French)

shore: Riva, River (French)

short nosed: Courtney (French)

shrine: Sher (English)

shy: Lajila (Hindi), Shyla (English)

sign: Nissa, Shanisa (Hebrew), Seema (Greek)

sign or symbol: Siete (Latin)

silence: Tacita (Latin)

silk: Silika (Tongan)

silky: Lene, Lenice (Latin)

silver: Ariana, Eirian (Welsh), Gin, Gina (Japanese), Silvia (Tongan), Silvana (Italian), Silvia (Latin)

sincere: Dyllis (Welsh)

singer: Gala (Norwegian), Minowa (Native American), Shadya

(Arabic), Yedda (English)

singled out: Vailea (German)

siren: Cryena, Sibena, Xirena (Greek), Laka (Hawaiian), Lora, Loree, Lorelei (Latin), Lori, Luraline, Lurline (German), Lorielle (French)

sister: Cissy, Sissy (English),

sky: Harah, Loila (Aboriginal), Kalani, Lani (Hawaiian), Vyoma (Hindi),

sky blue: Azura (Spanish)

sleep well: Louam (Ethiopian)

sleeping: Dorma (Latin)

sleeping child: Umina (Aboriginal)

sleepy: Lulie (English)

slender: Kaylee (Gaelic), Mwinwen (Welsh), Rewa (Polynesian)

slender branch: Dalit (Hebrew)

slim: Caley (Irish)

slim and fair: Cayla (Irish)

slow pace: Tamath (Arabic)

slow water: Shanita (Celtic)

small: Marmion (French), Paula, Paulette, Paulina, Pauline (Latin)

small beauty: Callula (Latin)

small bell: Nola, Nolana (Latin)

small bird: Jena (Arabic)

small crossing: Cantara (Arabic)

small field: Ohara (Japanese)

small hill: Tally (Hebrew)

small noble one: Edlyn (English)

small one: Ayesha (Persian)

small river: Ria (Spanish)

small sword: Gladys (Latin)

small town: Villette (French)

small waterfalls: Jirakee (Aboriginal)

small winged one: Alida (Latin)

smart woman: Eli (Sanskrit)

smile: Kanda (Kurdish)

smile of truth: Maimi (Japanese)

smiling a little: Koemi (Japanese)

smooth: Lenis, Lenita (Latin), Satin (French), Terentia (Greek)

smooth brow: Malvina (Gaelic)

snow: Eira (Welsh), Haukea (Hawaiian), Isatas (North American), Kumana (Aboriginal), Neige (French)

snowbird: Chilail (Native American)

snowdrop: Eiralys (Welsh)

soaring like a hawk: Iolana (Hawaiian)

soft: Lene, Lenice, Lenis, Lenita (Latin), Melba (Greek)

soft fur: Sable (English)

soft haired: Santillana (Spanish)

soft song: Myra (French)

soft touch: Caress (French)

soft violet colour: Mauve (Greek)

softness: Lamis (Arabic)

soldier: Armina, Armine (German)

solemn: Salina, Solana, Solenne (French)

solitary: Chalonna, Lona, Lone (Latin), Loni (English), Monica (Greek)

solitary angel: Alona (Latin)

some gift: Sunniva (Scandinavian)

someone from New Zealand: Mauli (Maori)

someone who worked in a monastery: Abbey (Scottish)

son of mighty warrior: Madison (English)

son of the little trueful one: Alison, Allison (Irish)

song: Aria (Italian), Carmen, Scharmaine (Latin), Chantara (American), Gita (Sanskrit), Hiva (Tongan), Melody (Greek), Odele, Shanta, Shantrice (French), Renni, Zemira (Hebrew)

song field: Utano (Japanese)

song of happiness: Sharice, Sharleen (French)

song of joy: Renata, Romola (Hebrew)

songbird: Sisika, Sora (Native American)

sorceress: Alcina (Greek), Rhiannon (Gaelic)

sorrow: Deisie, Dolores, Lolita (Spanish)

sorrowful: Dede (Welsh), Deidre (Irish), Delores (Spanish), Laraina, Laraine (Latin), Tristabelle (French)

sorrowful wander: Dedra (Irish)

sorrows: Lola (Spanish)

sound: Kani (Hawaiian)

Sound of tumbling water: Bondi (Aboriginal)

south wind: Coolalie (Aboriginal)

southerly wind: Sudy (English), Svea (Swedish)

Southern Cross constellation: Mirbabrook (Aboriginal), Toloa (Tongan)

sparkling: Amaryllis, Marney, Marnina (Greek), Seiran (Welsh)

speaker: Nata (Native American),

speaker from the meadow: Oralee (English)

speakers who you cannot understand: Cheyenne (Native American)

speaking: Junee (Aboriginal)

speaking sweetly: Olalla (Greek)

speaks sweetly: Ulalia (Greek)

spear carrier: Garyn (English)

spear ruler: Geralyn (German)

special: Elita (Latin)

spell: Jinx (Latin)

spice: Cassia (Greek), Levona, Livona (Hebrew)

spider: Hina (Tongan)

spiny: Acacia (Greek)

spirit of life: Enid (Welsh)

spirit of the night: Lilis (Hebrew)

spirited: Elana (Slavic)

splendid: Maja (Arabic)

splendor: Hadara (Hebrew)

Spring: Jarmilla (Slavic)

spring like: Verna (Latin)

spring of life: Kelda (Scandinavian)

springtime: Anastasia, Stacey, Stacia (Greek), Cerelia, Cerella (Latin)

square pillar made of stone: Herma (Latin)

squirrel: Salali (Native American)

stalking wolf: Takota (Native American)

star: Asta (Greek), Calca (Aboriginal), Estee, Esther (Persian), Hoshi (Japanese), Starla (English), Tannis (Gaelic), Astra, Astria, Astrid, Sidra, Stella, Vestah (Latin), Zwetlana (Russian)

star constellation: Vela (Latin)

star light: Svetlana (Russian)

star like: Asta, Astera, Asteria (Greek), Etoile (French),

star of the sea: Landa, Leire, Mairi, Marian, Mariana, Marilla,

Marilyn, Marion, Miri, Miriam, Polly, Pollyana (Hebrew), Maire (Irish), Manka, Marjan (Polish), Manon (French), Manette, Marfa, Mary, Maryanne, Marybeth, Maryellen, Maryjo, Marylou, Molly (Latin), Manya (Russian), Marabel, Maribella, Marice (English), Mariel, Markia (Dutch), Marja (Finnish), Maroula (Greek), Maruca, Marushka (Spanish), Mhairie (Scottish)

star system: Galaxy (Latin)

starling bird: Starling (English)

stay near: Kalyan (Aboriginal)

steadfast: Ethana (Hebrew)

steady: Petrina (Greek)

stem: Vanda (German)

stone: Chantal, Chantelle, Shantelle, Shantille (French), Hanya (Aboriginal), Peita, Peta, Pernella, Petra, Pierette (Greek), Perilla (Latin), Sela (Hebrew)

stork: Koko (Japanese)

storm: Jurisa (Slavic), Tempany (Latin), Tempest (French)

storyteller: Rawiya (Arabic)

straight: Kyle (Irish), Sarala (Hindi)

stranger: Barbara (Latin), Basha (Polish), Galla (Celtic), Varina (Russian)

stranger or foreign woman: Basia (Polish)

stream: Derora (Greek), Rilla (German)

stream from which water gushes: Waikiki (Hawaiian)

street: Rudra (French)

strength: Bridget, Meagan, Megan (Irish), Bryga (Polish), Drusilla, Val, Valancia, Valene, Valli (Latin), Kaoru (Japanese), Malohi (Tongan), Melecent (German), Mena (Dutch), Obelia (Greek), Veera (Hindi)

strength of God: Gabriella, Gabrielle, Gaby (Italian)

strength of right-hand: Yesima (Hebrew)

strength three times over: Mio (Japanese)

strength through the battle: Tilda (German)

strengthen and comfort: Comfort (English)

strife for wealth: Ede (English)

striving: Amalea, Amaline (German),

strong: Abira, Adira, Ethana (Hebrew), Alima (Arabic), Andria, Andriana, Valentina, Valentine, Valerie, Valonia, Valora (Latin), Bernice (Greek), Breana, Bria, Byanna (Celtic), Anrette, Arnelle, Bernadette, Bernadine (French), Carlotta (Italian), Charla (English), Charmaine (German), Lera (Russian), Valencia (Spanish), Waleria (Polish)

strong brave bear: Bernadette, Bernadine (German)

strong herbs: Rudra (English)

strong like a lioness: Lenice (German)

strong minded: Alcina (Greek), Imala (North American)

strong or courageous: Carol (German), Corolann, Carolina, Caroline (German)

strong powerful warrior: Matilda (German), Maud (French)

strong princess: Valentia (Latin)

strong property: Edrice (English)

strong spear: Gertrude, Truda, Trudy (German)

strong spirit: Brita, Britt, Britta (Irish)

strong victory: Bree (Irish)

strong willed: Mitzi (German), Miriam (Hebrew)

strong woman: Carla (English), Lita, Lola (Spanish)

strong worker: Millicent (German)

stutter: Blaise (Latin)

style: Flair (English)

successful: Nailah (Arabic)

successful hunter: Sunki (Native American),

sugar: Sato (Japanese), Suka (Tongan)

summer: Sya, Chinese, ,

sun: Cyra, Kyra, Takina (Persian), Idalia (Spanish), Kala (Hawaiian), Kalinda (Sanskrit), Ravva (Hindi)

sun angel: Solana (French)

sun god: Surya (Pakistani)

sun ray: Elle (Greek), Nell, Nellie (Latin), Yeira (Russian)

sun shower: Uha-tea (Tongan)

sunflower: Chamania (Hebrew), Nanala (Hawaiian), Soleil (French)

sunlight: Apoline, Pola (Greek), Solenne (Spanish)

sunray: Elaine, Eleanor, Helen, Helena (Greek)

sunrise: Bara (Aboriginal), Dawn (English), Usha (Sanskrit)

sunshine: Solada (Spanish), Zelene (English)

superior: Lois (Greek)

swamp: Sawa (Japanese)

swan: Helsa (English)

sweet: Adonica (Spanish), Candy, Honey (English), Ceinlys (Welsh), Dulcie, Elysia, Malinda, Melinda, Mindy (Latin), Kadla (Aboriginal), Malie (Tongan), Mel (Portuguese), Pam (Greek), Sakara (Native American), Sato (Japanese)

sweet basil herb: Rihana (Arabic)

sweet faced: Anika, Anneka (African)

sweet flower: Kamilia (Slavic)

sweet friend: Malvina (Latin)

sweet lady: Vevina (Gaelic)

sweet like honey: Melissa (Greek), Melosa (Spanish), Missy (English), Velika (Latin)

sweet little one: Miette (French)

sweet marjoram: Mejorana (Spanish)

sweet natured: Priya (Latin)

sweet potato: Kumala (Tongan)

sweet singing bird: Efrona (Hebrew)

sweet smelling flower: Kakala (Tongan), Reyhan (Polynesian)

sweet smelling tree: Chan (Cambodian)

sweet valley: Avoca (Irish)

sweet wine: Portia (Latin)

sweetcorn: Maisie (French)

sweetheart: Novia (Spanish)

sweetly scented: Olinda (Latin)

sweetly scented flower: Petunia (Native American)

swift: Fleta (German), Sunki (Native American)

swift bird: Aya (Hebrew)

swiftly moving arrow: Terrene (Japanese)

sword: Brenda (Norse), Zeva (Greek)

sword friend: Melva, Melvina, Merva (English)

symbol: Seema (Greek)

T

tailor: Taylor (English)

taken from the water: Moesha (Hebrew), Moselle, Mosina (French)

talented: Sahar (Japanese), Tabia (Swahili)

talk: Lallie (English)

talkative: Callan (German), Lalirra (Aboriginal), Lalita (Greek)

talking water: Vailea (Polynesian)

tall as the heavens: Semira (Hebrew)

tame: Damaris (Greek)

tamed: Damiana (Greek)

tasteful: Hao (Vietnamese)

teacher: Dido (Greek)

temple: Miya (Japanese), Templa (Latin)

temptress: Jalena, Taleisha (Latin)

tender: Bilhah, Mahalia (Hebrew), Caress (French), Ghada (Arabic), Jin (Japanese), Malva, Terentia (Greek), Minna (German)

tender touch: Charis, Charissa, Charisse (French)

thankful: Jendaya (Zimbabwean), Shakira (Arabic)

the beginning: Conchita (Spanish)

the best: Kimi (Japanese)

the challenger's descendant: Delany (Irish)

the coming moon: Magena (North American)

the meadow replacer: Jamilee (Hebrew)

the moon: Diana, Diane (Latin),

the morning: Lamorna (English)

the morning star: Ladancia (French)

the mother of the gods: Ladana (Finnish)

the people: Cambria (Welsh)

the queen: Laquinta (English)

the sea: Moana (Tongan)

the song is mine: Liron (Hebrew)

the woods: Laketa (Scottish)

their haired: Jennifer (English)

there: Lissilma (Native American)

thinker: Raissa (French)

thirsting for the truth: Ita (Gaelic)

this year: Ceara (Gaelic)

thistle: Cynara (Greek)

thorn: Acacia (Greek), Barbara, Vardis (English)

thorny bush: Briar (English)

thorny cactus: Sabara (Hebrew)

thread: Nima (Hebrew)

three: Trinity (Latin)

three arrows: Miya (Japanese)

three trees growing together: Miki (Japanese)

thunder: Thora (Scandinavian)

thunder bolt: Nari (Japanese)

tiger: Taika (Tongan), Tora (Japanese)

tile layer: Tyler (English)

timekeeper: Horatia (Latin), Orazia (Italian)

tired: Lea, Leah, Leigh (Hebrew)

to bind: Rita, Riva (Hebrew)

to cry out: Callan (Norse)

to cut: Taylor (English)

to fill: Ulla (French)

to gaze: Shamira (Spanish)

to give in: Jenelle (English)

to increase: Czenzi (Hungarian)

to love: Esme (French)

to open: Avril (Latin)

to proclaim: Demelda (Greek)

to rise: Levania (Latin)

to select: Bara (Hebrew)

to test: Nissa (Hebrew)

to touch: Helki (North American)

to waken: Wakenda (Norse)

today: Jilli (Aboriginal)

together: Unity (English)

tomorrow: Combara (Aboriginal)

towards the east: Kedma (Hebrew)

tower: Alena (Hebrew)

trader: Yarmilla (Slavic)

tranquil: Siri (Scandinavian), Xerena (Latin)

treasure: Koloa (Tongan), Lakia (Arabic)

treasured: Ozara (Hebrew)

tree: Eilah (Hebrew), Elana, Ilana (Hebrew), Karmiti (African), Randa (Arabic), Salato (Tongan)

tree bark: Kiri, Kirianne

tree bark by the pool of water: Kirilina (Maori)

tree branch: Dalya (Hebrew)

tribe of the Vandals: Waleria (Slavic)

triumph: Falzah, Zafina (Arabic)

trojan: Iliana (Greek)

true: Dyllis (Welsh), Fay (French)

true image: Veronica (Latin), Walaniki (Hawaiian)

trustworthy: Falala (Tongan), Honesta (Latin)

truth: Asha (Persian), Dilys (Welsh), Vera, Verena (Latin)

truth is gracious: Verdiana (Latin)

truth or truthful one: Alethea (Greek)

truthful: Alice, Alicia (Greek), Alvera, Veronica (Latin), Amita (Hebrew), Verita, Verity, Verona (Italian), Vreneli (German), Wera (Polish)

truthful child: Maeko (Japanese)

truthful one or truth: Alethea (Greek)

tulip flower: Lala (Slavic)

turbulent: Tempest (French)

turtle: Kame (Japanese)

twilight: Ata (Tongan), Sandyha (Hindi)

twin: Germina (Greek), Tamasina, Tamassa (Aramaic), Tameka, Tasida, Tasmin (Hebrew)

twisted willows: Pat (Native American)

twisting vine: Bryony (English)

U

ultimate bliss: Ananda (Sanskrit)

uncertain: Lynette (French)

under the skies of peace: Malulani (Hawaiian)

understanding: Bina (Hebrew), Lakendra (English)

unexpected gift or guest: Halla (Swahili)

unity: Ona (Latin), Sumati (Hindi)

universal battle: Imelda (German)

universal harmony: Cosima (Greek)

unknown: Shakeia, Shakia (African)

unpredictable destiny: Lila (Hindi)

unseeing: Secelia, Seelia (Latin)

untamed: Wilda (English)

used to: Solita (Latin)

V

vain: Vanity (English)

valiant: Riley, Rylee (Irish)

valley: Dahlia, Dena (English), Tangia (Japanese)

very attractive: Adonia (Greek)

very beautiful: Vashti (Persian)

victorious: Faizah (Arabic)

victorious: Jaia, Jaya (Hindi), Jayne (Sanskrit), Shina (Japanese)

victorious one: Latoya (Spanish)

victorious ship: Kelsey (English)

victory: Lari, Lora, Loree, Lorelei, Loren, Lorena, Lorenza, Lori, Lorice, Lorina, Lorina, Lorissa, Lorna, Vicki, Vicky, Victoria (Latin), Latoya, Loris (Spanish), Vika (Polynesian), Vittoria (Italian), Wikolia (Hawaiian), Wisia (Polish), Loricia (Greek), Kelila (Hebrew)

victory bringer: Bernice (Greek)

victory of the people: Nakeita, Nakia, Nikita (Russian), Nichelle (French), Nicki, Nicky, Nicola, Nicole (Greek)

view: Bakana, Kalinda (Aboriginal)

Viking goddess of fate: Norna (Norse)

village: Mura (Japanese)

vine branch: Vidonia (Portuguese)

vineyard: Carmela (Hebrew), Vina, Vinita (Spanish)

violet: Indigo (Latin), Ione (Greek)

violet color or flower: Viola, Violanie, Violante, Violet (Latin),

Violetta (Latin)

violet colored: Ianthe (Greek)

violet colored flower: Iola (Greek)

violet flower: Fiala (Slavic), Ianthe, Iolanda (Greek), Jolan, Hungarian, Yalande, Yola, Yolanda (Greek)

virgin: Ginny (Latin), Karida, Fadila (Arabic)

virtuous: Oretha (Greek)

virtuous strength: Rianna (Irish)

visible: Delia (Greek)

vision: Aissa (Gaelic)

visionary: Idola (Greek)

voice: Vani (Hindi)

voyager: Trixi, Trixie (Latin)

W

waiting: Talena (Tongan)

walk: Lalaka (Tongan)

wall: Dixie (English)

walrus: Ualusi (Tongan)

wanderer: Gypsy (English)

wanderer: Lawanda, Shawanna, Wanda (German)

wandering: Dessa (Greek), Faren (English), Tawanna (German)

war: Alnaba (Native American), Kelly (Irish)

war heroine: Griselda (German)

war-like: Marcella, Marcena, Marcia, Marcie, Martina (Latin), Markeisha, Markie (Swahili)

warm: Calida (Spanish)

warm and friendly: Bladina (Latin)

warm hearted: Cordella (Latin)

warrior: Armina, Dustine, Hilda, Imelda, Waida (German), Avice (French), Bernice (Greek), Bodil (Norse), Earlene (English), Bernia, Marcella, Marcena, Marcia, Marcie, Martina, Vernice (Latin), Kelly, Shakela (Irish), Manda (Spanish), Markeisha, Markie (Swahili), Sloane (Scottish), Toyah, Tracey, Tracie (Gaelic), Tyra (Scandinavian)

warrior who wears a bracelet in battle: Armilla (Latin)

watcher: Somoriah (Hebrew)

watchful: Casey (Gaelic), Grischa (Russian), Ira (Hebrew), Theora (Greek)

watchtower: Atalaya (Arabic)

water: Moree (Aboriginal)

water fairy: Shalonda (Latin)

water hen: Kilkie (Aboriginal)

water jug: Jarita (Arab)

water possum: Leena (Aboriginal)

water spring: Curra (Aboriginal)

waterfall: Sarila (Turkish), Taki (Japanese)

water lily: Arika (Aboriginal)

waterside: Lindsay (English)

wave: Nami (Japanese)

wave of water: Ondine (Latin)

weak: Claudia (French)

wealth: Clover (English), Ozara (Hebrew)

wealthy: Ashira, Jesse, Jessica, Jessie, Lajessica, Yessica (Hebrew), Daria (Greek), Darielle (Persian), Edrea, Uda, Udele (English), Elodie (Latin), Etenia (Native American), Gessica (Italian), Jessamine (French), Jezebel, Ujana (Spanish), Odelia (Scandinavian), Sakae, Sakura, Tomi (Japanese), Yusra, Zaidee (Arabic)

wealthy friend: Edwina (English)

wealthy gift: Dita (Slavic)

wealthy one from the pool: Jessalin (Hebrew)

wealthy protector: Edmee, Edna (English)

wealthy ruler: Edris (English)

wealthy ruling guardian: Teddi (English)

weapon used for protection: Wapeka (Norse)

weaver: Peneli, Penelope, Penny (Greek)

welcome: Orana (Aboriginal)

welcomed: Xena (Greek)

well born: Gena (Greek)

well by the place near the fountain spring: Kelby (Scandinavian)

well fed: Sedna (Eskimo)

well loved: Doda (Hebrew)

well spoken: Effie, Eulalia, Lali, Reza (Greek)

well-behaved: Rei (Japanese)

well-being: Ola (Nigerian)

West: Nishi (Japanese)

where the waters meet: Bombala (Aboriginal)

white: Alba, Albina, Alva (Latin), Beca, Becky, Bela (Slavic), Bianca (Italian), Blanca, Neva, Vianca (Spanish), Blanche, Genevieve (French), Elva, Elvie, Elvy (Irish), Gwen, Gwenda, Jenny (Welsh), Ivory (English), Lewanna (Hebrew), Wendy (Welsh)

white and smooth: Gayna (Welsh)

white box tree: Berry (Aboriginal)

white cow: Boann (Irish)

white eyes: Mrena (Slavic)

white flower: Puakea (Hawaiian)

white footprints: Olwyn (Welsh)

white friend: Rhonwen (Celtic)

white glow: Candy (Latin)

white haired: Jenna (Welsh)

white light: Galina (Russian)

white like the moon: Livana (Hebrew)

white oak: Byhalia (Native American)

white rose: Rosalba (Latin)

white shouldered: Finola (Gaelic)

white shoulders: Nola, Nolana (Gaelic)

white skin: Oriella (Celtic)

white skinned: Wenda (Welsh)

white stone: Izusa (North American)

white water: Whitney (English)

white wave: Genna, Ginnifer, Jennifer (English), Jinny, Vanora (Welsh), Vevetta, Vevette (French)

white wave from the meadow: Jenilee (Welsh)

white wave in the pool: Jennalyn (English)

wholesome: Althea (Greek)

wicked: Jezebel (Hebrew)

wide awake girl: Onawa (Native American)

wife of the moon: Inas (Polynesian)

wife of Zeus: Hera (Greek)

wild: Thera (Greek)

wild flower: Kawana (Aboriginal)

wild mountain goat: Jael (Hebrew)

wilful: Billie (English), Thelma (Greek)

wilful: Ulema, Velma, Vilhelmina, Vilhelmine (German), Vilma (Dutch), Iva (Russian)

willow tree: Kai (Native American), Willow (English)

wind: Makani (Hawaiian), Myrrine (Aboriginal)

wind of spring: Mayra (Aboriginal)

wind of the South: Kareela (Aboriginal)

wind over a bubbling stream: Iuana (Native American)

wine: Lora, Loree, Lorelei, Vinia (Latin)

winged: Aleta (Latin)

winner: Fayza (Arabic)

Winter: Fuyu (Japanese), Koleyn (Aboriginal)

wisdom: Benah, Dara, Jada (Hebrew), Darah, Ismena, Minerva (Greek)

wisdom: Rhiamon (Welsh), Saffi (Danish), Sappi (Lithuanian), Sofia, Sonia, Sophie (Greek), Sophia (French), Ulema (Arabic), Veda (Sanskrit), Veleda (German), Vye (African), Zofia (Slavic), Zophie (Bohemian)

wise: Alda (German), Aubery (French), Elrida (English), Kyna (Irish), Sage (Latin)

wise counsel: Conradine (German)

wise counsellor: Monique (French)

wise protector: Ramona (Spanish)

wise woman: Sevilla (Spanish), Sibyl (Greek)

wish: Mouna (Arabic)

wish which is fulfilled: Neylan (Turkish)

wished for: Landa, Leire, Mairi, Marian, Mariana, Marilla, Marilyn, Marion, Marla, Marlee, Miri, Miriam (Hebrew), Maire (Irish), Manya (Russian), Marabel, Maribella (English), Marfa (Latin), Mariel, Markia (Dutch), Marja (Finnish), Marjan (Polish), Maroula (Greek), Maruca, Marushka (Spanish), Mhairie (Scottish)

wishing: Molly (Hebrew)

with the grace of God: Zaneta (Hebrew)

wolf: Zeta (Hebrew)

woman: Cai (Vietnamese), Femi (French), Isha, Nekeisha, Rohini (Hindi), Sheila (Australian), Unna (Icelandic), Zana, Zemira (Persian), Keohi (Hawaiian), Kumari, Mahila (Sanskrit), Lotta (Swedish), Mahla (Native American), Lakeisha, Laneisha, Lekasha, Leneisha, Liesha, Nissa, Quaneisha, Shalana, Talise, Yiesha (Arabic), Maia, Maida, Mayda (English), Mima (Burmese), Nakeisha (Arabic)

woman chief: Winema (Native American)

woman from Sheba: Saarah (Greek)

woman of honor: Nora (Latin)

woman of my country: Utina (Native American)

woman of power: Mahala (Native American)

woman of respect: Siti (Swahili)

woman of the people: Leoda (Greek), Leota (German)

woman warrior: Bathilda (German), Gunda (Norwegian)

women: Betulah (Hebrew)

women from the sea: Narelle (Aboriginal)

wonder: Tamah (Hebrew)

wonderful: Lelei (Tongan), Mira, Mirabel, Mireil (Latin), Seki (Japanese)

wonderful: Shameka (Latin)

wonderful gift: Ediva (English)

wood of arrows: Wahkuna (Native American)

wooden drum: Lali (Tongan)

woods: Silika (Latin)

wool: Laine, Lainey (French)

woolly: Lana, Lanni (Latin)

work: Amaline (German), Hana (Hawaiian)

worker in the field: Orino (Japanese)

worshipper of the sun: Saura (Hindi)

worth gold: Orva (French)

worthy of admission: Rana (Latin)

worthy of love: Mabel, Mandy, Maybell, Miranda (Latin)

worthy of the Lord: Iola (Welsh)

woven silk: Aya (Japanese)

wreath of flowers: Vija (Latvian)

wren: Lirra (Aboriginal)

wren bird: Wrena (English)

wrote: Sass (Irish)

Y

Yahweh is just: Adalia (Hebrew)

yearly crops: Anona (Latin)

yellow: Blaine (Gaelic), Kaneli (Tongan), Saffron (Arabic)

yellow brown color: Hazel (English)

yellow flower: Alyssa (Greek), Kal (English)

yellow flowering plant: Celandine (Greek)

young: Ghada (Arabic), Hebe (Greek), Yula (Russian)

young archer: Evette, Lavonna, Yvette (French)

young bird: Gillian (Latin)

young ceremonial attendant: Cami, Camilla, Camille, Camille (French)

young child: Colina (Irish), Paige (English)

young deer: Afina, Ophra, Oprah (Hebrew)

young fairy queen: Kortanya (Russian)

young gazelle: Rasha (Arabic)

young girl: Kanya (Sanskrit), Kolina (Swedish), Korena, Kortina (Greek)

young lioness: Kefria (Hebrew)

young unmarried woman: Mada, Maddie, Madeleine, Madge (Hebrew)

young woman: Kamballa (Aboriginal)

youngest child: Avara (Sanskrit), Ayesha (Arabic)

youthful: Gillian, Jill, Jillaine, Jillian, Julene, Julia, Julie, Novia, Sulia, Yulene (Latin), Neola (Greek), Yulia (Russian)

youthful grace: Juliana (Slavic)
youthful warrior: Evania (Irish)

Printed in Great Britain
by Amazon.co.uk, Ltd.,
Marston Gate.